Consecrated Life

Vita Consecrata

ANNIVERSARY EDITION

Consecrated Life

Vita Consecrata

ANNIVERSARY EDITION

POPE JOHN PAUL II

With commentary by Marianne Lorraine Trouvé, FSP

BOOKS & MEDIA

Boston

Library of Congress Cataloging-in-Publication Data

Catholic Church. Pope (1978-2005 : John Paul II)

[Vita consecrata. English]

Consecrated life / Saint Pope John Paul II ; with commentary by Marianne Lorraine Trouvé, FSP. -- Anniversary edition.

pages cm

Translation of Vita consecrata.

Includes bibliographical references.

ISBN 978-0-8198-1647-4 -- ISBN 0-8198-1647-7

1. Monastic and religious life--Papal documents. 2. Catholic Church--Clergy--Religious life--Papal documents. I. John Paul II, Pope, 1920-2005. II. Trouvé, Marianne Lorraine. III. Title.

BX2435.C3613 2014

255--dc23

2014025304

The Scripture quotations contained in the commentary are from the *New Revised Standard Version Bible: Catholic Edition*, copyright © 1989, 1993, Division of Christian Education of the National Council of the Churches of Christ in the United States of America. Used by permission. All rights reserved.

Cover design by Rosana Usselmann

Cover photo by Mary Emmanuel Alves, FSP

"P" and PAULINE are registered trademarks of the Daughters of St. Paul.

Text of *Vita Consecrata* © Libreria Editrice Vaticana, 00120, Cittá del Vaticana. Used with permission. All rights reserved.

Published by Pauline Books & Media, 50 Saint Pauls Avenue, Boston, MA 02130-3491

Printed in the U.S.A.

www.pauline.org

Pauline Books & Media is the publishing house of the Daughters of St. Paul, an international congregation of women religious serving the Church with the communications media.

1 2 3 4 5 6 7 8 9   19 18 17 16 15

Contents

�֍

CHAPTER I

Confessio Trinitatis: The Origins of the Consecrated Life

Preface

A few years ago some sisters in my community had a book fair at a nearby Catholic school. One fourth grade boy, looking quite serious, approached the table and asked the sister, "Are you a nun?"

"Yes," she replied.

He pondered this for a moment and then said, "I didn't think they existed anymore. I saw one once when I was in kindergarten, but I thought they were extinct by now."

It may indeed seem like nuns are an endangered species today. But despite this little boy's assessment, in fact they are not. The Church will never be without sisters, brothers, and members of other forms of the consecrated life. In *Vita Consecrata*, Pope John Paul II gives reasons for hope that this life will continue not only to exist in the Church, but also to flourish.

The Apostolic Exhortation on Consecrated Life, *Vita Consecrata*, has an important place in the program that John Paul II developed. This document can best be seen in light of the Pope's double purpose: first, to continue to implement the renewal that Vatican II had called for, and second, to prepare the Church for the third millennium of the Christian era.

From the beginning of his pontificate, John Paul II was focused on the new millennium. He wrote, "Preparing for the *Year 2000 has become as it were a hermeneutical key of my Pontificate*" (*Tertio Millennio Adveniente*, no. 23). John Paul II was convinced that the world was ripe for a new evangelization. He was concerned about the whole world, both those areas in which the Gospel proclamation was still new, and those areas that had formerly been Christian but where many people had fallen away from the practice of the faith. His efforts to implement the teachings of Vatican II were a way of preparing the Church to carry out the new evangelization more fruitfully.

Part of this preparation consisted of the series of synods held on various topics, one of them being the consecrated life. That Synod was held at Rome in October 1994. In *Vita Consecrata*, John Paul II presented the fruits of the synod to the entire Church. While *Vita Consecrata* can be read with great profit on its own, it can be best understood in the context of his overall teaching. In terms of the consecrated life, that teaching can be found especially in three sources: in the document *Redemptionis Donum* (*To Men and Women Religious on Their Consecration in the Light of the Mystery of the Redemption*, March 25, 1984), in the general audiences on consecrated life that John Paul II gave during the Synod (which he mentions in *Vita Consecrata*, no. 13), and in his teaching on the theology of the body. Although the theology of the body focuses especially on marriage, in it John Paul II also gave a shorter but profound teaching on the meaning of "continence for the Kingdom of heaven." Both vocations are like two sides of the same coin. Both are rooted in what he called the spousal nature of the body and of the human person, and both spring from a complete gift of self. These themes can be found woven throughout the text of *Vita Consecrata*.

Before reading the text in detail, it is helpful to have an overall view of the document. It consists of a brief introduction, three chapters, and a conclusion. The three chapters focus on consecration, communion, and mission. The first chapter is the most theologically weighty, the most challenging to read—and the most rewarding. John Paul II considers the consecrated life in relation to the Trinity, using the Gospel scene of the transfiguration. In this chapter he makes an extremely profound statement, one that could change our whole way of viewing the consecrated life. Speaking of the three evangelical counsels of chastity, poverty, and obedience, John Paul II says that the way Jesus lived these "appears as the most radical way of living the Gospel on this earth, a way which may be called *divine*, for it was embraced by him, God and man, as the expression of his relationship as the Only-Begotten Son with the Father and with the Holy Spirit" (no. 18). Think about that—in living as he did, Jesus was living out his relationship with the other Persons of the Trinity. To follow him in this way of life is to be drawn into the communion that he, as the Son, had with the Father and the Holy Spirit, and to be drawn into it in a unique way. That thought alone gives us much to ponder.

In chapter two, John Paul II focuses on communion of life as a way of participating in the wider life of the Church seen as a communion. This "spirituality of communion" (no. 46) is a challenge to all those in the consecrated life, whether or not they live in a community. It is another way to reflect the Trinity, which is a communion of Persons. As human persons, we are the image of God not only because we are rational beings, with reason and free will, but also because we form relationships with other persons. As John Paul II said in *Redemptionis Donum*, "Vocation carries with it the answer to the question: Why be a human person—and how?" (no. 5). The "how" is closely tied to the quality of our relationships with others. Living in a community offers many opportunities to love and serve them by making a gift of ourselves.

In chapter three, the Pope considers the wide field of mission. The gift of self also extends to others in the wider world. Those in the consecrated life carry out an immense number of works. Mission also draws us deeper into the life of the Trinity even as we are sent out, for the Holy Spirit is the principal agent of mission (no. 72). For those in the consecrated life, mission leads to a spiritual fruitfulness, one marked by the Spirit. While they give up having children of their own, they give life to others in so many different ways. Whether they teach, wipe a tear from a child's eye, offer a hot meal to a hungry person, or console someone grieving the death of a loved one, consecrated persons witness to the love of Jesus Christ in our midst. In all this, they also witness to eternal life to come, what John Paul II calls the eschatological nature of this vocation. They can bring hope even into seemingly hopeless situations, because they bring the promise of Christ who said, "I am the way, and the truth, and the life" (Jn 14:6).

In this new edition of *Vita Consecrata*, a brief commentary follows each part of the document and includes an invitation to ponder, to pray, and to act.[*] Many passages in *Vita Consecrata* could be used very fruitfully for prayer and meditation. If you like the Ignatian method of imaginative prayer, you could envision yourself on Tabor with the apostles, contemplate the radiant face of Jesus, and listen for the words he is saying to you. But in whatever way you pray, the words of Saint John Paul offer a sure way to enter more deeply into the life of the Blessed Trinity and to make that life fruitful in whatever mission God has entrusted to you.

---

[*] The document has three chapters, each with several parts. The commentary covers each part separately, except where two shorter parts are combined (Chapter 2, parts two and three; and Chapter 3, parts three and four).

Topical Outline

POST-SYNODAL APOSTOLIC
EXHORTATION
OF THE HOLY FATHER
JOHN PAUL II

Consecrated Life

Vita Consecrata

To the Bishops and Clergy, Religious Orders
and Congregations, Societies of Apostolic Life,
Secular Institutes, and All the Faithful
On the Consecrated Life and Its Mission
in the Church and in the World

Introduction

1. The consecrated life, deeply rooted in the example and teaching of Christ the Lord, is a gift of God the Father to his Church through the Holy Spirit. By the profession of the evangelical counsels *the characteristic features of Jesus*—the chaste, poor, and obedient one—*are made constantly "visible" in the midst of the world*, and the eyes of the faithful are directed toward the mystery of the Kingdom of God already at work in history, even as it awaits its full realization in heaven.

In every age there have been men and women who, obedient to the Father's call and to the prompting of the Spirit, have chosen this special way of following Christ, in order to devote themselves to him with an "undivided" heart (cf. 1 Cor 7:34). Like the apostles, they too have left everything behind in order to be with Christ and to put themselves, as he did, at the service of God and their brothers and sisters. In this way, through the many charisms of spiritual and apostolic life bestowed on them by the Holy Spirit, they have helped to make the mystery and mission of the Church shine forth, and in doing so have contributed to the renewal of society.

Thanksgiving for the consecrated life

2. Because the role of consecrated life in the Church is so important, I decided to convene a Synod in order to examine in depth its significance and its future prospects, especially in view of the approaching new millennium. It was my wish that the Synodal Assembly should include, together with the bishops, a considerable number of consecrated men and women, in order that they too might contribute to the common reflection.

We are all aware of the treasure which the gift of the consecrated life, in the variety of its charisms and institutions, represents for the ecclesial community. *Together let us thank God* for the religious orders and institutes devoted to contemplation or the works of the apostolate, for societies of apostolic life, for secular institutes and for other groups of consecrated persons, as well as for all those individuals who, in their inmost hearts, dedicate themselves to God by a special consecration.

The Synod was a tangible sign of the universal extension of the consecrated life, present in the local Churches throughout the world. The consecrated life inspires and accompanies the spread of evangelization in the different parts of the world, where institutes from abroad are gratefully welcomed and new ones are being founded, in a great variety of forms and expressions.

Consequently, although in some parts of the world institutes of consecrated life seem to be experiencing a period of difficulty, in other places they are prospering with remarkable vitality. This shows that the choice of total self-giving to God in Christ is in no way incompatible with any human culture or historical situation. Nor is the consecrated life flourishing within the Catholic Church alone. In fact, it is particularly vibrant in the monasticism of the Orthodox Churches, where it is an essential feature of their life. It is also taking root or re-emerging in the Churches and Ecclesial Communities which originated in the Reformation, and is the sign of a grace shared by all of Christ's disciples. This fact is an incentive to ecumenism, which fosters the desire for an ever-fuller communion between Christians, "that the world may believe" (Jn 17:21).

The consecrated life: a gift to the Church

3. Its universal presence and the evangelical nature of its witness are clear evidence—if any were needed—that the consecrated life *is not something isolated and marginal*, but a reality which affects the whole Church. The bishops at the Synod frequently reaffirmed this: *"de re nostra agitur,"* "this is something which concerns us all."[1] In effect, *the consecrated life is at the very heart of the Church* as a decisive element for her mission, since it "manifests the inner nature of the Christian calling'"[2] and the striving of the whole Church as Bride toward union with her one Spouse.[3] At the Synod it was stated on several occasions that the consecrated life has not only proved a help and support for the Church in the past, but is also a precious and necessary gift for the present and future of the People of God, since it is an intimate part of her life, her holiness and her mission.[4]

The present difficulties which a number of institutes are encountering in some parts of the world must not lead to a questioning of the fact that the profession of the evangelical counsels is *an integral part of the Church's life* and a much needed incentive toward ever greater fidelity to the Gospel.[5] The consecrated life may experience further changes in its historical forms, but there will be no change in the substance of a choice which finds expression in a radical gift of self for love of the Lord Jesus and, in him, of every member of the human family. This certainty, which has inspired countless individuals in the course of the centuries, continues to reassure the Christian people, for they know that they can draw from the contribution of these generous souls powerful support on their journey toward the heavenly home.

Gathering the fruits of the Synod

4. In response to the desire expressed by the Ordinary General Assembly of the Synod of Bishops which met to discuss the theme "The Consecrated Life and Its Mission in the Church and in the World," I intend to set forth in this Apostolic Exhortation the results of the Synod process[6] and to point out to all the faithful—bishops, priests, deacons, consecrated persons, and laity, and to any others who might be interested—the wondrous things which today too the Lord wishes to accomplish through the consecrated life.

This Synod, coming after the ones dedicated to the lay faithful and to priests, completes the treatment of the distinctive features of the states of life willed by the Lord Jesus for his Church. Whereas the Second Vatican Council emphasized the profound reality of ecclesial communion, in which all gifts converge for the building up of the Body of Christ and for the Church's mission in the world, in recent years there has been felt the need to clarify the specific identity of the various states of life, their vocation, and their particular mission in the Church.

Communion in the Church is not uniformity, but a gift of the Spirit who is present in the variety of charisms and states of life. These will be all the more helpful to the Church and her mission the more their specific identity is respected. For every gift of the Spirit is granted in order to bear fruit for the Lord[7] in the growth of fraternity and mission.

The work of the Spirit in the various forms of the consecrated life

5. How can we not recall with gratitude to the Spirit *the many different forms of consecrated life* which he has raised up throughout history and which still exist in the Church today? They can be compared to a plant with many branches[8] which sinks its roots into the Gospel and brings forth abundant fruit in every season of the Church's life. What an extraordinary richness! I myself, at the conclusion of the Synod, felt the need to stress this permanent element in the history of the Church: the host of founders and foundresses, of holy men and women who chose Christ by radically following the Gospel and by serving their brothers and sisters, especially the poor and the outcast.[9] Such service is itself a sign of how the consecrated life manifests the organic unity of the commandment of love, in the inseparable link between love of God and love of neighbor.

The Synod recalled this unceasing work of the Holy Spirit, who in every age shows forth the richness of the practice of the evangelical counsels through a multiplicity of charisms. In this way too he makes ever present in the Church and in the world, in time and space, the mystery of Christ.

Monastic life in the East and the West

6. The Synod Fathers from the Eastern Catholic Churches and the representatives of the other Churches of the East emphasized *the evangelical values of monastic life*,[10] which appeared at the dawn of Christianity and which still flourishes in their territories, especially in the Orthodox Churches.

From the first centuries of the Church, men and women have felt called to imitate the Incarnate Word who took on the condition of a servant. They have sought to follow him by living in a particularly radical way, through monastic profession, the demands flowing from baptismal participation in the Paschal Mystery of his death and resurrection. In this way, by becoming bearers of the cross (*staurophoroi*), they have striven to become bearers of the Spirit (*pneumatophoroi*), authentically spiritual men and women, capable of endowing history with hidden fruitfulness by unceasing praise and intercession, by spiritual counsels and works of charity.

In its desire to transfigure the world and life itself in expectation of the definitive vision of God's countenance, Eastern monasticism gives pride of place to conversion, self-renunciation, and compunction of heart, the quest for *hesychia* or interior peace, ceaseless prayer, fasting and vigils, spiritual combat and silence, paschal joy in the presence of the Lord and the expectation of his definitive coming, and the oblation of self and personal possessions, lived in the holy communion of the monastery or in the solitude of the hermitage.[11]

The West too from the first centuries of the Church has practiced the monastic life and has experienced a great variety of expressions of it, both cenobitic and eremetical. In its present form, inspired above all by Saint Benedict, Western monasticism is the heir of the great number of men and women who, leaving behind life in the world, sought God and dedicated themselves to him, "preferring nothing to the love of Christ."[12] The monks of today likewise strive to *create a harmonious balance between the interior life and work* in the evangelical commitment to conversion of life, obedience, and stability, and in persevering dedication to meditation on God's word (*lectio divina*), the celebration of the liturgy, and prayer. In the heart of the Church and the world, monasteries have been and continue to be eloquent signs of communion, welcoming abodes for those seeking God and the things of the spirit, schools of faith and true places of study, dialogue, and culture for the building up of the life of the Church and of the earthly city itself, in expectation of the heavenly city.

The Order of Virgins; hermits and widows

7. It is a source of joy and hope to witness in our time a new flowering of *the ancient Order of Virgins*, known in Christian communities ever since apostolic times.[13] Consecrated by the diocesan bishop, these women acquire a particular link with the Church, which they are committed to serve while remaining in the world. Either alone or in association with others, they constitute a *special eschatological image of the*

Heavenly Bride and of the life to come, when the Church will at last fully live her love for Christ the Bridegroom.

Men and women hermits, belonging to ancient orders or new institutes, or being directly dependent on the bishop, bear witness to the passing nature of the present age by their inward and outward separation from the world. By fasting and penance, they show that man does not live by bread alone but by the word of God (cf. Mt 4:4). Such a life "in the desert" is an invitation to their contemporaries and to the ecclesial community itself *never to lose sight of the supreme vocation*, which is to be always with the Lord.

Again being practiced today is the consecration of *widows*,[14] known since apostolic times (cf. 1 Tim 5:5, 9–10; 1 Cor 7:8), as well as the consecration of widowers. These women and men, through a vow of perpetual chastity as a sign of the Kingdom of God, consecrate their state of life in order to devote themselves to prayer and the service of the Church.

Institutes completely devoted to contemplation

8. Institutes completely devoted to contemplation, composed of either women or men, are for the Church a reason for pride and a source of heavenly graces. By their lives and mission, the members of these institutes imitate Christ in his prayer on the mountain, bear witness to God's lordship over history, and anticipate the glory which is to come.

In solitude and silence, by listening to the word of God, participating in divine worship, personal asceticism, prayer, mortification, and the communion of fraternal love, they direct the whole of their lives and all their activities to the contemplation of God. In this way they offer the ecclesial community a singular testimony of the Church's love for her Lord, and they contribute, with hidden apostolic fruitfulness, to the growth of the People of God.[15]

Thus there is good reason to hope that the different forms of contemplative life will experience *continued growth in the younger Churches* as an evident sign that the Gospel has taken firm root, especially in those areas of the world where other religions predominate. This will make it possible to bear witness to the vitality of the traditions of Christian asceticism and mysticism and will contribute to interreligious dialogue.[16]

Apostolic religious life

9. The West has also known, down the centuries, a variety of other expressions of religious life, in which countless persons, renouncing the world, have consecrated themselves to God through the public profession of the evangelical counsels in accordance with a specific charism and in a stable form of common life,[17] *for the sake of carrying out different forms of apostolic service to the People of God.* Thus there arose the different families of canons regular, the mendicant orders, the clerics regular, and in general the religious congregations of men and women devoted to apostolic and missionary activity and to the many different works inspired by Christian charity.

This is a splendid and varied testimony, reflecting the multiplicity of gifts bestowed by God on founders and foundresses who, in openness to the working of the Holy

Spirit, successfully interpreted the signs of the times and responded wisely to new needs. Following in their footsteps, many other people have sought by word and deed to embody the Gospel in their own lives, bringing anew to their own times the living presence of Jesus, the consecrated one *par excellence*, the one sent by the Father. In every age consecrated men and women must continue to be images of Christ the Lord, fostering through prayer a profound communion of mind with him (cf. Phil 2:5–11), so that their whole lives may be penetrated by an apostolic spirit and their apostolic work with contemplation.[18]

Secular institutes

10. The Holy Spirit, who wondrously fashions the variety of charisms, has given rise in our time to *new expressions of consecrated life*, which appear as a providential response to the new needs encountered by the Church today as she carries out her mission in the world.

One thinks in the first place of members of *secular institutes* seeking to *live out their consecration to God in the world* through the profession of the evangelical counsels in the midst of temporal realities; they wish in this way to be a leaven of wisdom and a witness of grace within cultural, economic, and political life. Through their own specific blending of presence in the world and consecration, they seek *to make present in society the newness and power of Christ's Kingdom*, striving to transfigure the world from within by the power of the Beatitudes. In this way, while they belong completely to God and are thus fully consecrated to his service, their activity in the ordinary life of the world contributes, by the power of the Spirit, to shedding the light of the Gospel on temporal realities. Secular institutes, each in accordance with its specific nature, thus help to ensure that the Church has an effective presence in society.[19]

A valuable role is also played by *clerical secular institutes*, in which priests who belong to the diocesan clergy, even when some of them are recognized as being incardinated in the institute, consecrate themselves to Christ through the practice of the evangelical counsels in accordance with a specific charism. They discover in the spiritual riches of the institute to which they belong great help for living more deeply the spirituality proper to the priesthood, and thus they are enabled to be a leaven of communion and apostolic generosity among their fellow clergy.

Societies of apostolic life

11. Also worthy of special mention are *societies of apostolic life* or of common life, composed of men or women. These pursue, each in its own particular way, a specific apostolic or missionary end. In many of them an explicit commitment to the evangelical counsels is made through sacred bonds officially recognized by the Church. Even in this case, however, the specific nature of their consecration distinguishes them from religious institutes and secular institutes. The specific identity of this form of life is to be preserved and promoted; in recent centuries it has produced many fruits of holiness and of the apostolate, especially in the field of charity and in the spread of the Gospel in the missions.[20]

New expressions of consecrated life

12. The perennial youth of the Church continues to be evident even today. In recent years, following the Second Vatican Council, *new or renewed forms of the consecrated life* have arisen. In many cases, these are institutes similar to those already existing, but inspired by new spiritual and apostolic impulses. Their vitality must be judged by the authority of the Church, which has the responsibility of examining them in order to discern the authenticity of the purpose for their foundation, and to prevent the proliferation of institutions similar to one another, with the consequent risk of a harmful fragmentation into excessively small groups. In other cases it is a question of new experiments which are seeking an identity of their own in the Church and awaiting official recognition from the Apostolic See, which alone has final judgment in these matters.[21]

These new forms of consecrated life now taking their place alongside the older ones bear witness to the constant attraction which the total gift of self to the Lord, the ideal of the apostolic community and the founding charisms continue to exert, even on the present generation. They also show how the gifts of the Holy Spirit complement one another.

In this newness, however, the Spirit does not contradict himself. Proof of this is the fact that the new forms of consecrated life have not supplanted the earlier ones. Amid such wide variety the underlying unity has been successfully preserved, thanks to the one call to follow Jesus—chaste, poor, and obedient—in the pursuit of perfect charity. This call, which is found in all the existing forms of consecrated life, must also mark those which present themselves as new.

Purpose of the Apostolic Exhortation

13. Gathering together the fruits of the Synod's labors, in this Apostolic Exhortation I wish to address the whole Church in order to offer not only to consecrated persons but also to the bishops and the faithful *the results of a stimulating exchange*, guided by the Holy Spirit with his gifts of truth and love.

During these years of renewal, the consecrated life, like other ways of life in the Church, has gone through a difficult and trying period. It has been a period full of hopes, new experiments, and proposals aimed at giving fresh vigor to the profession of the evangelical counsels. But it has also been a time of tension and struggle, in which well-meaning endeavors have not always met with positive results.

The difficulties, however, must not lead to discouragement. Rather, we need to commit ourselves with fresh enthusiasm, for the Church needs the spiritual and apostolic contribution of a renewed and revitalized consecrated life. In this Post-Synodal Exhortation, I wish to address religious communities and consecrated persons in the same spirit which inspired the letter sent by the Council of Jerusalem to the Christians of Antioch, and I am hopeful that it will meet with the same response: "When they read it, they rejoiced at the encouragement which it gave" (Acts 15:31). And not only this. I also hope to increase the joy of the whole People of God. As they become better acquainted with the consecrated life, they will be able with greater awareness to thank Almighty God for this great gift.

In an attitude of heartfelt openness toward the Synod Fathers, I have carefully considered the valuable contributions made during the intense work of the Assembly, at which I made a point of being present throughout. During the Synod, I also sought to offer the entire People of God a number of systematic talks on the consecrated life in the Church. In them I presented anew the teachings found in the texts of the Second Vatican Council, which was an enlightening point of reference for subsequent doctrinal developments and for the reflections of the Synod during the busy weeks of its work.[22]

I am confident that the sons and daughters of the Church, and consecrated persons in particular, will receive this Exhortation with open hearts. At the same time, I hope that reflection will continue and lead to a deeper understanding of the great gift of the consecrated life in its three aspects of consecration, communion, and mission. I also hope that consecrated men and women, in full harmony with the Church and her Magisterium, will discover in this Exhortation further encouragement to face in a spiritual and apostolic manner the new challenges of our time.

PONDER

Two themes stand out as John Paul II begins his document: thanksgiving and gift. The consecrated life is a wonderful gift of God to the Church, and it calls for a profound sense of thanksgiving. This gift is so important that the Church can never be without it. In fact, "consecrated life is at the very heart of the Church" (no. 3). The grace that accompanies the gift of religious consecration is always at work in those whom God calls to this vocation. In their turn, religious are enabled to make a gift of self that springs from a radical love of Jesus Christ. When they do this and live out their vocation well, they make Jesus visible to the world. Consecrated persons may be found everywhere—helping the poor, the sick, the forgotten, the lonely—sharing Christ's mercy and compassion with all people.

John Paul II focuses on positive signs of renewal and speaks of some new forms of consecrated life that have been developing since the Second Vatican Council. Yet he does not ignore the difficulties either. He recognizes that consecrated life "has gone through a difficult and trying period . . . a time of tension and struggle" (no. 13). In relation to consecrated life, the winds of change that swept through the Church after Vatican II were more like a tornado than a gentle breeze. Religious sisters in particular welcomed the renewal that the Council called for and took important steps to implement it. Yet along with needed updating and expanding into new forms of mission, problems began to appear. Many members left, vocations dried up, and some institutes had to cut back on their apostolic works. As one religious sister whom I met at a retreat put it, "I feel like I've been living an experiment for the past forty years!"

But that wasn't the whole picture. As the Pope mentions, the situation varied in different parts of the world. By the time Pope John Paul II wrote *Vita Consecrata* in 1996, other, newer forms of consecrated life had also begun to take root and to grow. The Holy Spirit was at work amid the ferment and continues to inspire new charisms in the Church. Among other forms of consecrated life, the Pope mentions monastic life, the order of virgins, contemplative institutes, apostolic religious life, secular institutes, and societies of apostolic life. New foundations have been made, and while not all of these will endure, they testify to the vitality of the consecrated life.

Despite the many challenges that remain, John Paul II intends to offer encouragement and hope. As the history of the Church has shown, times of renewal and flourishing have often followed times of difficulty. While we don't know exactly how things will unfold, we do know that Jesus will be with us just as he was with the apostles in the storm on the lake. He will continue to invite generous persons to "go, sell what you own, and give the money to the poor, and you will have treasure in heaven; then come, follow me" (Mk 10:21).

1. What do you know about the consecrated life from your own experience? In your own part of the world, do you see more shadows or lights? Even if shadows seem to

predominate, what signs of hope do you see for consecrated life?

2. Pope John Paul II lists a number of different forms of the consecrated life. Which forms are you most familiar with, and in what ways? How do you see the Holy Spirit at work in them?

3. *Vita Consecrata* begins with the statement, "The consecrated life, deeply rooted in the example and teaching of Christ the Lord, is a gift of God the Father to his Church through the Holy Spirit." As you read the document, look for ways that the Pope continues to develop this Trinitarian approach. What is your own understanding of how each Person of the Trinity is present and active in the consecrated life?

4. In the Introduction, Pope John Paul II uses some terminology that relates to the theology of the body, such as his references to the gift of self, Christ the Bridegroom, and the spousal nature of the Church. Each human person is called to love, and so live out the spousal meaning of the body. How does this enrich our view of the vocation to marriage as well as the vocation to continence for the sake of the Kingdom?

PRAY

Pope John Paul II addressed this document to the whole Church. Perhaps you are already settled in your own vocation, whether in marriage or the consecrated life. Or perhaps you are still searching for the path God is calling you to follow. In either case, you could use the following prayer to live well one's own vocation, written by Blessed James Alberione, SSP, the founder of the Pauline Family.

> Heavenly Father, I believe in your wisdom and love. I believe you created me for heaven, marked out for me the way to reach it, and await me there to give me the reward of the faithful servant. Give me light and show me this way. Grant me the strength to follow it generously. I ask this of you, through Jesus Christ, your Son, and through Mary, my Queen and Mother. At the moment of death, may I be able to say with St. Paul: "I have finished the course. I have fought the good fight. Now there is laid up for me the crown of the just" (see 2 Tim 4:7–8). Amen.

Act

Many Catholics are familiar with the consecrated life because of the sisters who taught them in parochial schools. Perhaps you know such a sister or religious brother or priest who had a positive impact on your life. If so, you might consider writing a thank you letter either to that person or to his or her congregation (you could find the contact information online). If that is not practical, you could offer some prayers for them instead.

Confessio Trinitatis

The Origins of the Consecrated Life in the Mystery of Christ and of the Trinity

Icon of the Transfigured Christ

14. The evangelical basis of consecrated life is to be sought in the special relationship which Jesus, in his earthly life, established with some of his disciples. He called them not only to welcome the Kingdom of God into their own lives, but also to put their lives at its service, leaving everything behind and closely imitating his own *way of life*.

Many of the baptized throughout history have been invited to live such a life "in the image of Christ." But this is possible only on the basis of a special vocation and in virtue of a particular gift of the Spirit. For in such a life baptismal consecration develops into a radical response in the following of Christ through acceptance of the evangelical counsels, the first and essential of which is the sacred bond of chastity for the sake of the Kingdom of Heaven.[23] This special way of "following Christ," at the origin of which is always the initiative of the Father, has an essential Christological and pneumatological meaning; it expresses in a particularly vivid way the *Trinitarian* nature of the Christian life and it anticipates in a certain way that *eschatological* fulfillment toward which the whole Church is tending.[24]

In the Gospel, many of Christ's words and actions shed light on the meaning of this special vocation. But for an overall picture of its essential characteristics, it is singularly helpful to fix our gaze on Christ's radiant face in the mystery of the transfiguration. A whole ancient spiritual tradition refers to this "icon" when it links the contemplative life to the prayer of Jesus "on the mountain."[25] Even the "active" dimensions of consecrated life can in a way be included here, for the transfiguration is not only the revelation of Christ's glory but also a preparation for facing Christ's cross. It involves both "going up the mountain" and "coming down the mountain." The disciples who have enjoyed this intimacy with the Master, surrounded for a moment by the splendor of the Trinitarian life and of the communion of saints, and as it were caught up in the horizon of eternity, are immediately brought back to daily reality, where they see "Jesus only," in the lowliness of his human nature, and are invited to return to the valley, to share with him the toil of God's plan and to set off courageously on the way of the cross.

"And he was transfigured before them . . ."

15. *And after six days Jesus took with him Peter and James and John his brother, and led them up a high mountain apart. And he was transfigured before them, and his face shone like the sun,*

and his garments became white as light. And behold, there appeared to them Moses and Elijah, talking with him. And Peter said to Jesus, "Lord, it is well that we are here; if you wish, I will make three booths here, one for you and one for Moses and one for Elijah." He was still speaking, when lo, a bright cloud overshadowed them, and a voice from the cloud said, "This is my beloved Son, with whom I am well pleased; listen to him." When the disciples heard this, they fell on their faces, and were filled with fear. But Jesus came and touched them, saying, "Rise, and have no fear." And when they lifted up their eyes, they saw no one but Jesus only.

And as they were coming down the mountain, Jesus commanded them, "Tell no one the vision, until the Son of man is raised from the dead" (Mt 17:1–9).

The event of the transfiguration *marks a decisive moment in the ministry of Jesus*. It is a revelatory event which strengthens the faith in the disciples' hearts, prepares them for the tragedy of the cross, and prefigures the glory of the resurrection. This mystery is constantly relived by the Church, the people on its way to the eschatological encounter with its Lord. Like the three chosen disciples, the Church contemplates the transfigured face of Christ in order to be confirmed in faith and to avoid being dismayed at his disfigured face on the cross. In both cases, she is the Bride before her Spouse, sharing in his mystery and surrounded by his light.

This light shines on all the Church's children. *All are equally called to follow Christ*, to discover in him the ultimate meaning of their lives, until they are able to say with the Apostle: "For to me to live is Christ" (Phil 1:21). But those who are called to the consecrated life have *a special experience of the light which shines forth from the Incarnate Word.* For the profession of the evangelical counsels makes them *a kind of sign and prophetic statement* for the community of the brethren and for the world; consequently they can echo in a particular way the ecstatic words spoken by Peter: "Lord, it is well that we are here" (Mt 17:4). These words bespeak the Christocentric orientation of the whole Christian life. But they also eloquently express the *radical* nature of the vocation to the consecrated life: how good it is for us to be with you, to devote ourselves to you, to make you the one focus of our lives! Truly those who have been given the grace of this special communion of love with Christ feel as it were caught up in his splendor: he is "the fairest of the sons of men" (Ps 45:2), the one beyond compare.

"This is my beloved Son": listen to him!

16. The three disciples caught up in ecstasy hear the Father's call to listen to Christ, to place all their trust in him, to make him the center of their lives. The words from on high give new depth to the invitation by which Jesus himself, at the beginning of his public life, called them to follow him, to leave their ordinary lives behind and to enter into a close relationship to him. It is precisely this special grace of intimacy which, in the consecrated life, makes possible and even demands the total gift of self in the profession of the evangelical counsels. The counsels, more than a simple renunciation, are *a specific acceptance of the mystery of Christ, lived within the Church.*

In the unity of the Christian life, the various vocations are like so many rays of the one light of Christ, whose radiance "brightens the countenance of the Church."[26] The *laity*, by virtue of the secular character of their vocation, reflect the mystery of the Incarnate Word particularly insofar as he is the Alpha and the Omega of the world, the foundation and measure of the value of all created things. *Sacred ministers*, for their part, are living images of Christ the Head and Shepherd who guides his people during this time of "already and not yet," as they await his coming in glory. It is the duty of the *consecrated life* to show that the Incarnate Son of God is *the eschatological goal toward which all things tend*, the splendor before which every other light pales, and the infinite beauty which alone can fully satisfy the human heart. In the consecrated life, then, it is not only a matter of following Christ with one's whole heart, of loving him "more than father or mother, more than son or daughter" (cf. Mt 10:37)—for this is required of every disciple—but of living and expressing this *by conforming one's whole existence to Christ* in an all-encompassing commitment which foreshadows the eschatological perfection, to the extent that this is possible in time and in accordance with the different charisms.

By professing the evangelical counsels, consecrated persons not only make Christ the whole meaning of their lives but strive to reproduce in themselves, as far as possible, "that form of life which he, as the Son of God, accepted in entering this world."[27] By embracing *chastity*, they make their own the pure love of Christ and proclaim to the world that he is the Only-Begotten Son who is one with the Father (cf. Jn 10:30, 14:11). By imitating Christ's *poverty*, they profess that he is the Son who receives everything from the Father and gives everything back to the Father in love (cf. Jn 17:7, 10). By accepting, through the sacrifice of their own freedom, the mystery of Christ's filial *obedience*, they profess that he is infinitely beloved and loving, as the one who delights only in the will of the Father (cf. Jn 4:34), to whom he is perfectly united and on whom he depends for everything.

By this profound "configuration" to the mystery of Christ, the consecrated life brings about in a special way that *confessio Trinitatis* which is the mark of all Christian life; it acknowledges with wonder the sublime beauty of God, Father, Son, and Holy Spirit, and bears joyful witness to his loving concern for every human being.

I. In Praise of the Trinity

"A Patre ad Patrem": God's initiative

17. Contemplation of the glory of the Lord Jesus in the icon of the transfiguration reveals to consecrated persons first of all the Father, the Creator and Giver of every good thing, who draws his creatures to himself (cf. Jn 6:44) with a special love and for a special mission. "This is my beloved Son: listen to him!" (cf. Mt 17:5). In response to this call and the interior attraction which accompanies it, those who are called entrust themselves to the love of God who wishes them to be exclusively at his service, and they consecrate themselves totally to him and to his plan of salvation (cf. 1 Cor 7:32–34).

This is the meaning of the call to the consecrated life: it is an initiative coming wholly from the Father (cf. Jn 15:16), who asks those whom he has chosen to respond with complete and exclusive devotion.[28] The experience of this gracious love of God is so deep and so powerful that the person called senses the need to respond by unconditionally dedicating his or her life to God, consecrating to him all things present and future, and placing them in his hands. This is why, with Saint Thomas, we come to understand the identity of the consecrated person, beginning with his or her complete self-offering, as being comparable to a genuine holocaust.[29]

"Per Filium": in the footsteps of the Son

18. The Son, who is the way which leads to the Father (cf. Jn 14:6), calls all those whom the Father has given to him (cf. Jn 17:9) to make the following of himself the whole purpose of their lives. But of some, those called to the consecrated life, he asks a total commitment, one which involves leaving everything behind (cf. Mt 19:27) in order to live at his side[30] and to follow him wherever he goes (cf. Rev 14:4).

In the countenance of Jesus, the "image of the invisible God" (Col 1:15) and the reflection of the Father's glory (cf. Heb 1:3), we glimpse the depths of an eternal and infinite love which is at the very root of our being.[31] Those who let themselves be seized by this love cannot help abandoning everything to follow him (cf. Mk 1:16–20; 2:14; 10:21, 28). Like Saint Paul, they consider all else as loss "because of the surpassing worth of knowing Jesus Christ," by comparison with which they do not hesitate to count all things as "refuse," in order that they "may gain Christ" (Phil 3:8). They strive to become one with him, taking on his mind and his way of life. This leaving of everything and following the Lord (cf. Lk

18:28) is a worthy program of life for all whom he calls, in every age.

The evangelical counsels, by which Christ invites some people to share his experience as the chaste, poor, and obedient one, call for and make manifest in those who accept them *an explicit desire to be totally conformed to him.* Living "in obedience, with nothing of one's own, and in chastity,"[32] consecrated persons profess that Jesus is the model in whom every virtue comes to perfection. His way of living in chastity, poverty, and obedience appears as the most radical way of living the Gospel on this earth, a way which may be called *divine,* for it was embraced by him, God and man, as the expression of his relationship as the Only-Begotten Son with the Father and with the Holy Spirit. This is why Christian tradition has always spoken of the *objective superiority of the consecrated life.*

Nor can it be denied that the practice of the evangelical counsels is also a particularly profound and fruitful way of sharing in *Christ's mission,* in imitation of the example of Mary of Nazareth, the first disciple, who willingly put herself at the service of God's plan by the total gift of self. Every mission begins with the attitude expressed by Mary at the Annunciation: "Behold, I am the handmaid of the Lord; let it be done to me according to your word" (Lk 1:38).

"In Spiritu": consecrated by the Holy Spirit

19. "A bright cloud overshadowed them" (Mt 17:5). A significant spiritual interpretation of the transfiguration sees this cloud as an image of the Holy Spirit.[33]

Like the whole of Christian life, the call to the consecrated life is closely linked to the working of the Holy Spirit. In every age, the Spirit enables new men and women to recognize the appeal of such a demanding choice. Through his power, they relive, in a way, the experience of the Prophet Jeremiah: "You have seduced me, LORD, and I have let myself be seduced" (Jer 20:7). It is the Spirit who awakens the desire to respond fully; it is he who guides the growth of this desire, helping it to mature into a positive response and sustaining it as it is faithfully translated into action; it is he who shapes and molds the hearts of those who are called, configuring them to Christ, the chaste, poor, and obedient one, and prompting them to make his mission their own. By allowing themselves to be guided by the Spirit on an endless journey of purification, they become, day after day, *conformed to Christ*, the prolongation in history of a special presence of the Risen Lord.

With penetrating insight, the Fathers of the Church have called this spiritual path *philokalia, or love of the divine beauty*, which is the reflection of the divine goodness. Those who by the power of the Holy Spirit are led progressively into full configuration to Christ reflect in themselves a ray of the unapproachable light. During their earthly pilgrimage, they press on toward the inexhaustible source of light. The consecrated life thus becomes a particularly profound expression of the Church as the Bride who, prompted by the Spirit to imitate her Spouse, stands before him "in splendor, without spot or wrinkle or any such thing, that she might be holy and without blemish" (Eph 5:27).

The same Spirit, far from removing from the life of humanity those whom the Father has called, puts them at the service of their brothers and sisters in accordance with their particular state of life, and inspires them to undertake special tasks in response to the needs of the Church and the world, by means of the charisms proper to the various institutes. Hence many different forms of the consecrated life have arisen, whereby the Church is "adorned by the various gifts of her children . . . like a bride made beautiful for her spouse (cf. Rev 21:2)"[34] and is enriched by the means necessary for carrying out her mission in the world.

The evangelical counsels, gift of the Trinity

20. The evangelical counsels are thus above all *a gift of the Holy Trinity*. The consecrated life proclaims what the Father, through the Son and in the Spirit, brings about by his love, his goodness, and his beauty. In fact, "the religious state reveals the transcendence of the Kingdom of God and its requirements over all earthly things. To all people it shows wonderfully at work within the Church the surpassing greatness of the force of Christ the King and the boundless power of the Holy Spirit."[35]

The first duty of the consecrated life is to *make visible* the marvels wrought by God in the frail humanity of those who are called. They bear witness to these marvels not so much in words as by the eloquent language of a transfigured life, capable of amazing the world. To people's astonishment they respond by proclaiming the wonders of grace accomplished by the Lord in those whom he loves. To the degree that consecrated persons let themselves be guided by the Spirit to the heights of perfection, they can exclaim: "I see the beauty of your grace, I contemplate its radiance, I reflect its light; I am caught up in its ineffable splendor; I am taken outside myself as I think of myself; I see how I was and what I have become. O wonder! I am vigilant, I am full of respect for myself, of reverence and of fear, as I would be were I before you; I do not know what to do, I am seized by fear, I do not know where to sit, where to go, where to put these members which are yours; in what deeds, in what works shall I use them, these amazing divine marvels!"[36] The consecrated life thus becomes one of the tangible seals which the Trinity impresses upon history, so that people can sense with longing the attraction of divine beauty.

Reflection of Trinitarian life in the evangelical counsels

21. The deepest meaning of the evangelical counsels is revealed when they are viewed in relation to the Holy Trinity, the source of holiness. They are in fact an expression of the love of the Son for the Father in the unity of the Holy Spirit. By practicing the evangelical counsels, the consecrated person lives with particular intensity the Trinitarian and Christological dimension which marks the whole of Christian life.

The *chastity* of celibates and virgins, as a manifestation of dedication to God with *an undivided heart* (cf. 1 Cor 7:32–34), is a reflection of the *infinite love* which links the three Divine Persons in the mysterious depths of the life of the Trinity, the love to which the Incarnate Word bears witness even to the point of giving his life, the love "poured into our hearts through the Holy Spirit" (Rom 5:5), which evokes a response of total love for God and the brethren.

Poverty proclaims that God is man's only real treasure. When poverty is lived according to the example of Christ who, "though he was rich . . . became poor" (2 Cor 8:9), it becomes an expression of that *total gift of self* which the three Divine Persons make to one another. This gift overflows into creation and is fully revealed in the Incarnation of the Word and in his redemptive death.

Obedience, practiced in imitation of Christ, whose food was to do the Father's will (cf. Jn 4:34), shows the liberating beauty of a *dependence which is not servile but filial*, marked by a deep sense of responsibility and animated by mutual trust, which is a reflection in history of the loving *harmony* between the three Divine Persons.

The consecrated life is thus called constantly to deepen the gift of the evangelical counsels with a love which grows ever more genuine and strong in the *Trinitarian* dimension: love *for Christ*, which leads to closeness with him; love *for the Holy Spirit*, who opens our hearts to his inspiration; love *for the Father*, the first origin and supreme goal of the consecrated life.[37] The consecrated life thus becomes a confession and a sign of the Trinity, whose mystery is held up to the Church as the model and source of every form of Christian life.

Even *fraternal life*, whereby consecrated persons strive to live in Christ with "one heart and soul" (Acts 4:32), is put forward as an eloquent witness to the Trinity. It proclaims *the Father*, who desires to make all of humanity one family. It proclaims *the Incarnate Son*, who gathers the redeemed into unity, pointing the way by his example, his prayer, his words, and above all his death, which is the source of reconciliation for a divided and scattered humanity. It proclaims *the Holy Spirit* as the principle of unity in the Church, wherein he ceaselessly raises up spiritual families and fraternal communities.

Consecrated like Christ for the Kingdom of God

22. The consecrated life, through the prompting of the Holy Spirit, "constitutes a closer imitation and an abiding re-enactment in the Church"[38] of the way of life which Jesus, the supreme consecrated one and missionary of the Father for the sake of his Kingdom, embraced and proposed to his disciples (cf. Mt 4:18–22; Mk 1:16–20; Lk 5:10–11; Jn 15:16). In the light of Jesus' consecration, we can see in the initiative of the Father, the source of all holiness, the ultimate origin of the consecrated life. Jesus is the one whom "God anointed . . . with the Holy Spirit and with power" (Acts 10:38), the one "whom the Father consecrated and sent into the world" (Jn 10:36). Accepting his consecration by the Father, the Son in turn consecrates himself to the Father for the sake of humanity (cf. Jn 17:19). His life of virginity, obedience, and poverty expresses his complete filial acceptance of the Father's plan (cf. Jn 10:30; 14:11). His perfect offering confers an aspect of consecration upon all the events of his earthly existence.

Jesus is *the exemplar of obedience*, who came down from heaven not to do his own will but the will of the one who sent him (cf. Jn 6:38; Heb 10:5, 7). He places his way of living and acting in the hands of the Father (cf. Lk 2:49). In filial obedience, he assumes the condition of a servant: he "emptied himself, taking the form of a servant . . . and became obedient unto death, even death on a cross" (Phil 2:7–8). In this attitude of submissiveness to the Father, Christ lives his life as a virgin, even while affirming and defending the dignity and sanctity of married life. He thus reveals *the sublime excellence and mysterious spiritual fruitfulness of virginity*. His full acceptance of the Father's plan is also seen in his detachment from earthly goods: "though he was rich, yet for your sake he became poor, so that by his poverty you might become rich" (2 Cor 8:9). *The depth of his poverty* is revealed in the perfect offering of all that is his to the Father.

The consecrated life truly constitutes *a living memorial of Jesus' way of living and acting* as the Incarnate Word in relation to the Father and in relation to the brethren. It is a living tradition of the Savior's life and message.

PONDER

In this theologically rich chapter, John Paul II develops his teaching in light of the transfiguration. In the radiant face of Christ we can find the ultimate meaning and purpose of the consecrated life. The Pope stresses how the Trinity is involved in consecrated life. The Father takes the initiative. The Son, consecrated by the Father, in turn consecrates himself, and "his perfect offering confers an aspect of consecration upon all the events of his earthly existence" (no. 22). The Holy Spirit, as the bond of love between them, is active in bringing this about. Jesus takes up a way of life marked by chastity, poverty, and obedience. John Paul II calls this "the most radical way of living the Gospel on this earth, a way which may be called *divine*, for it was embraced by him, God and man, as the expression of his relationship as the Only-Begotten Son with the Father and with the Holy Spirit" (no. 18).

This is very profound. Jesus' way of life was how he, the Son, lived in communion with the Father and the Spirit during his earthly life. His life was Trinitarian to the core. And when Jesus invites others to follow him in this way of life, he is inviting them into a special relationship with the Trinity, one that is modeled on his own life. John Paul II says that "the consecrated life thus becomes a confession and a sign of the Trinity, whose mystery is held up to the Church as the model and source of every form of Christian life" (no. 21).

This brings us to a delicate question. In number 18, he speaks of "the objective superiority of the consecrated life." He uses the term again in number 32. What does he mean? He is not negating the teaching of Vatican II on the universal call to holiness in the Church. Before the Council, Catholics often thought of priests and religious as being called to a higher holiness than lay people. The great spiritual masters did not propose this view, but sometimes the popular understanding may have skewed that way. But all the baptized are called to holiness. John Paul II is not saying that consecrated persons are better or holier than the laity.

His talks on the theology of the body can shed light on this question. He notes that the "superiority" (his quotes) of continence for the sake of the Kingdom is to be understood in terms of its eschatological meaning. By giving up marriage and family, those called to this way of life give an eloquent testimony that our life on earth is not our whole reality. We look forward in hope to the coming of the Kingdom. He also stresses that we should not have any kind of Manichaean idea that would look down on marriage because of its relationship to the body and sex. He says, "The 'superiority' of continence to marriage never means, in the authentic tradition of the Church, a disparagement of marriage or a belittling of its essential value" (TOB 77.6).* Then he speaks about how marriage and continence are complementary vocations, both rooted in the spousal meaning of

---

* Quotations with the citation TOB are taken from John Paul II, *Man and Woman He Created Them*, trans. Michael Waldstein (Boston: Pauline Books & Media, 2006).

the body. He explains that meaning as: "*the power to express love: precisely that love in which the human person becomes a gift and—through this gift—fulfills the very meaning of his being and existence*" (TOB 15.1). While uniquely lived out in marriage, this spousal meaning is not limited to that state of life, but is expressed in all the ways we can make a gift of ourselves by loving and helping others.

In his theology of the body, John Paul II stresses the eschatological dimension of the consecrated life. He deepens that reflection in *Vita Consecrata* and speaks of the consecrated life as a way of showing forth the Church's holiness (see no. 32). This is based on a Trinitarian perspective. The Pope speaks of the inner reality of the form of life that Jesus himself lived and calls others to live. It is a unique participation in the life of the Trinity, a radical way of life. In number 16, John Paul II speaks of the different ways the various vocations in the Church reflect the light of Christ. He seems concerned to show the uniqueness of the consecrated life so that it will be better understood. After the Council, the decline of vocations could have been due, in part, to a misunderstanding of the universal call to holiness and a consequent blurring of the different vocations. John Paul II points out that the consecrated life differs not only from the priesthood but also from the lay life. In speaking of the excellence of consecrated life, he may have been trying to restore in the Church something that had gotten a bit lost after Vatican II.[*]

---

[*] For a further discussion of the meaning of the term "objective superiority," see Dennis J. Billy, CSSR, "Objective Superiority" in *Vita Consecrata, Review for Religious*, Nov–Dec 1996, pp. 640–645.

1. How does John Paul II's emphasis on the Trinitarian nature of the consecrated life help you to understand it better?

2. In going up the mountain we can glimpse something of the splendor of the Trinity that is at work in us. Yet in coming down the mountain we return to daily life, marked by the messiness of being human. How do you reconcile these two realities?

PRAY

Prayerfully read the account of the transfiguration (Mt 17:1–9; Mk 9:2–8; Lk 9:28–36). Imagine yourself in the scene as the three apostles were. What would you say to Jesus? What does he say to you?

ACT

John Paul II speaks of how the Spirit puts us at the service of our brothers and sisters (no. 19). What small, hidden task can you do to better serve others in your family or community?

II. Between Easter and Fulfillment

From Tabor to Calvary

23. The dazzling event of the transfiguration is a preparation for the tragic, but no less glorious, event of Calvary. Peter, James, and John contemplate the Lord Jesus together with Moses and Elijah, with whom, according to the Evangelist Luke, Jesus speaks "of his departure, which he was to accomplish at Jerusalem" (9:31). The eyes of the apostles are therefore fixed upon Jesus who is thinking of the cross (cf. Lk 9:43–45). There his virginal love for the Father and for all mankind will attain its highest expression. His poverty will reach complete self-emptying, his obedience the giving of his life.

The disciples are invited to contemplate Jesus raised up on the cross, where, in his silence and solitude, "the Word come forth from silence"[39] prophetically affirms the absolute transcendence of God over all created things; in his own flesh he conquers our sin and draws every man and every woman to himself, giving to all the new life of the resurrection (cf. Jn 12:32; 19:34, 37). It is in the contemplation of the crucified Christ that all vocations find their inspiration. From this contemplation, together with the primordial gift of the Spirit, all gifts, and in particular the gift of the consecrated life, take their origin.

After Mary, the Mother of Jesus, it is John who receives this gift. John is the disciple whom Jesus loved, the witness who together with Mary stood at the foot of the cross (cf. Jn 19:26–27). His decision to consecrate himself totally is the fruit of the divine love which envelops him, sustains him, and fills his heart. John, together with Mary, is among the first in a long line of men and women who, from the beginning of the Church until the end, are touched by God's love and feel called to follow the Lamb, once sacrificed and now alive, wherever he goes (cf. Rev 14:1–5).[40]

The Paschal dimension of the consecrated life

24. In the different forms of life inspired by the Spirit throughout history, consecrated persons discover that the more they stand at the foot of the cross of Christ, the more immediately and profoundly they experience the truth of God who is love. It is precisely on the cross that the one who in death appears to human eyes as disfigured and without beauty, so much so that the bystanders cover their faces (cf. Is 53:2–3), fully reveals the beauty and power of God's love. Saint Augustine says: "Beautiful is God, the Word with God. . . . He is beautiful in heaven, beautiful on earth; beautiful in the womb, beautiful in his parents' arms, beautiful in his miracles, beautiful in his sufferings; beautiful in inviting to life, beautiful in not worrying about death, beautiful in giving up his life and beautiful in taking it up again; he is beautiful on the cross, beautiful in the tomb, beautiful in heaven. Listen to the song with understanding, and let not the weakness of the flesh distract your eyes from the splendor of his beauty."[41]

The consecrated life reflects the splendor of this love because, by its fidelity to the mystery of the cross, it confesses that it believes and lives by the love of the Father, Son, and Holy Spirit. In this way it helps the Church to remain aware that *the cross is the superabundance of God's love poured out upon the world*, and that it is the great sign of Christ's saving presence, especially in the midst of difficulties and trials. This is the testimony given constantly and with deeply admirable courage by a great number of consecrated persons, many of whom live in difficult situations, even suffering persecution and martyrdom. Their fidelity to the one Love is revealed and confirmed in the humility of a hidden life, in the acceptance of sufferings for the sake of completing in their own flesh "what is lacking in Christ's afflictions" (Col 1:24), in silent sacrifice and abandonment to God's holy will, and in serene fidelity even as their strength and personal authority wane. Fidelity to God also inspires devotion to neighbor, a devotion which consecrated persons live out not without sacrifice by constantly interceding for the needs of their brothers and sisters, generously serving the poor and the sick, sharing the hardships of others and participating in the concerns and trials of the Church.

Witnesses to Christ in the world

25. The Paschal Mystery is also the wellspring of the Church's *missionary nature*, which is reflected in the whole of the Church's life. It is expressed in a distinctive way in the consecrated life. Over and above the charisms proper to those institutes which are devoted to the mission *ad gentes* or which are engaged in ordinary apostolic activity, it can be said that *the sense of mission is at the very heart of every form of consecrated life*. To the extent that consecrated persons live a life completely devoted to the Father (cf. Lk 2:49; Jn 4:34), held fast by Christ (cf. Jn 15:16; Gal 1:15–16) and animated

by the Spirit (cf. Lk 24:49; Acts 1:8; 2:4), they cooperate effectively in the mission of the Lord Jesus (cf. Jn 20:21) and contribute in a particularly profound way to the renewal of the world.

The first missionary duty of consecrated persons is to themselves, and they fulfill it by opening their hearts to the promptings of the Spirit of Christ. Their witness helps the whole Church to remember that the most important thing is to serve God freely, through Christ's grace which is communicated to believers through the gift of the Spirit. Thus they proclaim to the world the peace which comes from the Father, the dedication witnessed to by the Son, and the joy which is the fruit of the Holy Spirit.

Consecrated persons will be missionaries above all by continually deepening their awareness of having been called and chosen by God, to whom they must therefore direct and offer everything that they are and have, freeing themselves from the obstacles which could hinder the totality of their response. In this way they will become *true signs of Christ in the world.* Their lifestyle too must clearly show the ideal which they profess, and thus present itself as a living sign of God and as an eloquent, albeit often silent, proclamation of the Gospel.

The Church must always *seek to make her presence visible in everyday life*, especially in contemporary culture, which is often very secularized and yet sensitive to the language of signs. In this regard the Church has a right to expect a significant contribution from consecrated persons, called as they are in every situation to bear clear witness that they belong to Christ.

Since the habit is a sign of consecration, poverty, and membership in a particular Religious family, I join the Fathers of the Synod in strongly recommending to men and women religious that they wear their proper habit, suitably adapted to the conditions of time and place.[42] Where valid reasons of their apostolate call for it, religious, in conformity with the norms of their institute, may also dress in a simple and modest manner, with an appropriate symbol, in such a way that their consecration is recognizable.

Institutes which from their origin or by provision of their constitutions do not have a specific habit should ensure that the dress of their members corresponds in dignity and simplicity to the nature of their vocation.[43]

Eschatological dimension of the consecrated life

26. Since the demands of the apostolate today are increasingly urgent, and since involvement in temporal affairs risks becoming ever more absorbing, it is particularly opportune to draw attention once more to *the eschatological nature of the consecrated life.*

"Where your treasure is, there will your heart be also" (Mt 6:21). The unique treasure of the Kingdom gives rise to desire, anticipation, commitment, and witness. In the early Church, the expectation of the Lord's coming was lived in a particularly intense way. With the passing of the centuries, the Church has not ceased to foster this attitude of hope: she has continued to invite the faithful to look to the salvation which is waiting to be revealed, "for the form of this world is passing away (1 Cor 7:31; cf. 1 Pet 1:3–6)."[44]

It is in this perspective that we can understand more clearly *the role* of consecrated life as an *eschatological sign*. In fact it has constantly been taught that the consecrated life is a foreshadowing of the future Kingdom. The Second Vatican Council proposes this teaching anew when it states that consecration better "foretells the resurrected state and the glory of the heavenly Kingdom."[45] It does this above all by means of *the vow of virginity*, which tradition has always understood as *an anticipation of the world to come*, already at work for the total transformation of man.

Those who have dedicated their lives to Christ cannot fail to live in the hope of meeting him, in order to be with him for ever. Hence the ardent expectation and desire to "be plunged into the fire of love which burns in them and which is none other than the Holy Spirit,"[46] an expectation and desire sustained by the gifts which the Lord freely bestows on those who yearn for the things that are above (cf. Col 3:1).

Immersed in the things of the Lord, the consecrated person remembers that "here we have no lasting city" (Heb 13:14), for "our commonwealth is in heaven" (Phil 3:20). The one thing necessary is to seek God's "Kingdom and his righteousness" (Mt 6:33), with unceasing prayer for the Lord's coming.

Active expectation: commitment and watchfulness

27. "Come, Lord Jesus!" (Rev 22:20). This expectation is *anything but passive*: although directed toward the future Kingdom, it expresses itself in work and mission, that the Kingdom may become present here and now through the

spirit of the Beatitudes, a spirit capable of giving rise in human society to effective aspirations for justice, peace, solidarity, and forgiveness.

This is clearly shown by the history of the consecrated life, which has always borne abundant fruit even for this world. By their charisms, consecrated persons become signs of the Spirit pointing to a new future enlightened by faith and by Christian hope. *Eschatological expectation becomes mission*, so that the Kingdom may become ever more fully established here and now. The prayer "Come, Lord Jesus!" is accompanied by another: "Thy Kingdom come!" (Mt 6:10).

Those who vigilantly await the fulfillment of Christ's promises are able to bring hope to their brothers and sisters who are often discouraged and pessimistic about the future. Theirs is a hope founded on God's promise contained in the revealed word: the history of humanity is moving toward "a new heaven and a new earth" (Rev 21:1), where the Lord "will wipe away every tear from their eyes, and death shall be no more, neither shall there be mourning nor crying nor pain any more, for the former things have passed away" (Rev 21:4).

The consecrated life is at the service of this definitive manifestation of the divine glory, when all flesh will see the salvation of God (cf. Lk 3:6; Is 40:5). The Christian East emphasizes this dimension when it considers monks as *angels of God on earth* who proclaim the renewal of the world in Christ. In the West, monasticism is the celebration of memory and expectation: *memory* of the wonders God has wrought, and *expectation* of the final fulfillment of our hope. Monasticism and the contemplative life are a constant reminder that the primacy of God gives full meaning and joy to human lives, because men and women are made for God, and their hearts are restless until they rest in him.[47]

The Virgin Mary, model of consecration and discipleship

28. Mary is the one who, from the moment of her Immaculate Conception, most perfectly reflects the divine beauty. "All beautiful" is the title with which the Church invokes her. "The relationship with Mary most holy, which for every believer stems from his or her union with Christ, is even more pronounced in the life of consecrated persons. . . . Mary's presence is of fundamental importance both for the spiritual life of each consecrated person and for the solidity, unity, and progress of the whole community."[48]

Mary in fact is the *sublime example of perfect consecration*, since she belongs completely to God and is totally devoted to him. Chosen by the Lord, who wished to accomplish in her the mystery of the Incarnation, she reminds consecrated persons of *the primacy of God's initiative*. At the same time, having given her assent to the divine Word, made flesh in her, Mary is the *model of the acceptance of grace* by human creatures.

Having lived with Jesus and Joseph in the hidden years of Nazareth and present at her Son's side at crucial moments of his public life, the Blessed Virgin teaches unconditional discipleship and diligent service. In Mary, "the temple of the Holy Spirit,"[49] all the splendor of the new creation shines forth. Consecrated life looks to her as the sublime model of consecration to the Father, union with the Son, and openness to the Spirit, in the knowledge that acceptance of the "virginal and humble life"[50] of Christ also mean imitation of Mary's way of life.

In the Blessed Virgin Mary, consecrated persons also find *a Mother who is altogether unique*. Indeed, if the new motherhood conferred on Mary at Calvary is a gift for all Christians, it has a specific value for those who have completely consecrated their lives to Christ. "Behold your mother!" (Jn 19:27): Jesus' words to the disciple "whom he loved" (Jn 19:26) are particularly significant for the lives of consecrated persons. They, like John, are called to take the Blessed Virgin Mary to themselves (cf. Jn 19:27), loving her and imitating her in the radical manner which befits their vocation, and experiencing in return her special motherly love. The Blessed Virgin shares with them the love which enables them to offer their lives every day for Christ and to cooperate with him in the salvation of the world. Hence a filial relationship to Mary is the royal road to fidelity to one's vocation and a most effective help for advancing in that vocation and living it fully.[51]

PONDER

The apostles who witnessed Jesus at the transfiguration were also being schooled in the mystery of the cross. Coming down from Mount Tabor, Jesus would be led to climb Mount Calvary and die in great pain for the redemption of the world. Consecrated persons must also follow Jesus in his paschal mystery. John Paul II notes that in contemplating the crucified Christ "all vocations find their inspiration" (no. 23). In this section, the Pope introduces the theme of beauty connected with the cross. He uses a quotation from Saint Augustine that profoundly expresses the beauty of Christ on the cross, despite his marred and battered body.

This paschal dimension is also the root of "the sense of mission [that] is at the very heart of every form of consecrated life" (no. 25). Bathed in the love of Jesus that flows from the cross, the Church is impelled to go out to the world and invite others into that love. The many forms of mission are so many ways that Jesus continues to work in the world through the Holy Spirit to lead people to eternal life. John Paul II stresses that the eschatological dimension of the consecrated life does not hinder a sense of mission, but encourages it and makes it grow. This may seem like a paradox. Yet the thought of eternal life gives us hope. It makes everything we do on earth take on greater importance because it has very far-reaching consequences indeed.

In number 26, John Paul II speaks more about "the role of consecrated life as an eschatological sign" that shows forth the glory of the heavenly Kingdom. He adds, "It does this above all by means of *the vow of virginity*, which tradition has always understood as *an anticipation of the world to come*." The English translation here seems puzzling in its use of the word "vow." The official Latin has *virginalis electio*, which is better rendered as the choice or selection of virginity. The translations in other languages on the Vatican website also use the phrase "choice of virginity": *le choix de la virginité* (French), *la scelta verginale* (Italian), and *opción por la virginidad* (Spanish). "Choice of virginity" ties in better with the way John Paul II spoke in his theology of the body about those who are called to this vocation. They respond to God's call "in view of the particular value which is connected with this choice and which one must discover and welcome as one's own vocation" (TOB 73.3).

In making the choice for consecrated virginity, those called can look to Mary for support and encouragement. She is "the *sublime example of perfect consecration*" (no. 28). She is also the "all beautiful" one who stood at the foot of the cross and became our Mother in the order of grace.

1. While dying on the cross, Jesus said to the beloved disciple, "Behold your mother" (Jn 19:25). Jesus was inviting him, and by extension all of us through the ages, to welcome Mary into his life as a disciple. What role does Mary play in your spiritual life? What are some ways you could grow in your relationship with her?

2. In the Gospel, Jesus acknowledges that it is difficult to understand his call to some people to follow him by giving up marriage for the sake of the Kingdom. Do you see this call primarily as a renunciation, or also in terms of its positive value? In another place John Paul II says that those who make this choice can only do so because of the power that flows from the redemption of the body, won for us by Jesus Christ (see TOB 77.3, 4). Re-read number 24 of *Vita Consecrata*, which speaks of the paschal dimension of consecrated life. How does this relate to consecrated chastity?

3. John Paul II says that consecrated life points to the future Kingdom of God especially through the choice of consecrated chastity. How is this so? Does the hope of eternal life keep you going in difficult times? How does it inspire you to a deeper sense of mission?

Pray

"Consecrated persons discover that the more they stand at the foot of the cross of Christ, the more immediately and profoundly they experience the truth of God who is love" (no. 24). Take some time to pray quietly before the crucifix. If you are in any kind of pain, send it up to Jesus on the cross, asking him to take it to himself so that you are not suffering it alone but with him, for the sake of the Church (see Col 1:24). Then listen quietly for the healing word he may speak to your heart, whether it is a word of consolation, of encouragement, or of instruction. The word may not come right away, but eventually it will provide you with light.

ACT

John Paul II stresses how important it is for consecrated persons to free themselves "from the obstacles which could hinder the totality of their response" (no. 25). This requires insight into our own motives and desires. An excellent way of achieving insight is the daily practice of the examen prayer. Consider how you could make this practice part of your daily prayer if you are not already doing so.*

---

* See http://www.ignatianspirituality.com/ignatian-prayer/the-examen/con sciousness-examen/. An excellent resource is the book *The Examen Prayer: Ignatian Wisdom for Our Lives Today* by Timothy M. Gallagher, O.M.V., and the classic article by George Aschenbrenner, SJ, *The Consciousness Examen*.

III. In the Church and for the Church

"It is well that we are here": the consecrated life in the mystery of the Church

29. In the episode of the transfiguration, Peter speaks on behalf of the other apostles: "It is well that we are here" (Mt 17:4). The experience of Christ's glory, though completely filling his mind and heart, does not set him apart but rather unites him more closely to the "we" of the apostles.

This dimension of "we" invites us to consider the place which the consecrated life occupies in the *mystery of the Church*. In recent years, theological reflection on the nature of the consecrated life has deepened the new insights which emerged from the teaching of the Second Vatican Council. In the light of that teaching it has been recognized that the profession of the evangelical counsels *indisputably belongs to the life and holiness of the Church*.[52] This means that the consecrated life, present in the Church from the beginning, can never fail to be one of her essential and characteristic elements, for it expresses her very nature.

This is clearly seen from the fact that the profession of the evangelical counsels is intimately connected with the mystery of Christ, and has the duty of making somehow present the way of life which Jesus himself chose and indicated as an absolute eschatological value. Jesus himself, by calling some men and women to abandon everything in order to follow him, established this type of life which, under the guidance of the Spirit, would gradually develop down the centuries into the various forms of the consecrated life. The idea of a Church made up only of sacred ministers and lay people does not therefore conform to the intentions of her divine Founder, as revealed to us by the Gospels and the other writings of the New Testament.

New and special consecration

30. In the Church's tradition religious profession is considered to be *a special and fruitful deepening of the consecration received in Baptism*, inasmuch as it is the means by which the close union with Christ already begun in Baptism develops in the gift of a fuller, more explicit and authentic configuration to him through the profession of the evangelical counsels.[53]

This further consecration, however, differs in a special way from baptismal consecration, of which it is not a necessary consequence.[54] In fact, all those reborn in Christ are called to live out, with the strength which is the Spirit's gift, the chastity appropriate to their state of life, obedience to God and to the Church, and a reasonable detachment from material possessions: for all are called to holiness, which consists in the perfection of love.[55] But Baptism in itself does not include the call to celibacy or virginity, the renunciation of possessions, or obedience to a superior, in the form proper to the evangelical counsels. The profession of the evangelical counsels thus presupposes a particular gift of God not given to everyone, as Jesus himself emphasizes with respect to voluntary celibacy (cf. Mt 19:10–12).

This call is accompanied, moreover, by *a specific gift of the Holy Spirit*, so that consecrated persons can respond to their vocation and mission. For this reason, as the liturgies of the

East and West testify in the rite of monastic or religious profession and in the consecration of virgins, the Church invokes the gift of the Holy Spirit upon those who have been chosen and joins their oblation to the sacrifice of Christ.[56] The profession of the evangelical counsels is *also a development of the grace of the sacrament of Confirmation*, but it goes beyond the ordinary demands of the consecration received in Confirmation by virtue of a special gift of the Spirit, which opens the way to new possibilities and fruits of holiness and apostolic work. This can clearly be seen from the history of the consecrated life.

As for priests who profess the evangelical counsels, experience itself shows that *the Sacrament of Holy Orders finds a particular fruitfulness in this consecration*, inasmuch as it requires and fosters a closer union with the Lord. The priest who professes the evangelical counsels is especially favored in that he reproduces in his life the fullness of the mystery of Christ, thanks also to the specific spirituality of his institute and the apostolic dimension of its proper charism. In the priest, in fact, the vocation to the priesthood and the vocation to the consecrated life converge in a profound and dynamic unity.

Also of immeasurable value is the contribution made to the Church's life by religious priests completely devoted to contemplation. Especially in the celebration of the Eucharist they carry out an act of the Church and for the Church, to which they join the offering of themselves, in communion with Christ who offers himself to the Father for the salvation of the whole world.[57]

Relationships between the different states of Christian life

31. The different ways of life which, in accordance with the plan of the Lord Jesus, make up the life of the Church have mutual relationships which merit consideration.

By virtue of their rebirth in Christ, all the faithful share a common dignity; all are called to holiness; all cooperate in the building up of the one Body of Christ, each in accordance with the proper vocation and gift which he or she has received from the Spirit (cf. Rom 12:3–8).[58] The equal dignity of all members of the Church is the work of the Spirit, is rooted in Baptism and Confirmation, and is strengthened by the Eucharist. But diversity is also a work of the Spirit. It is he who establishes the Church as an organic communion in the diversity of vocations, charisms, and ministries.[59]

The vocations to the lay life, to the ordained ministry, and to the consecrated life can be considered paradigmatic, inasmuch as all particular vocations, considered separately or as a whole, are in one way or another derived from them or lead back to them, in accordance with the richness of God's gift. These vocations are also at the service of one another, for the growth of the Body of Christ in history and for its mission in the world. Everyone in the Church is consecrated in Baptism and Confirmation, but the ordained ministry and the consecrated life each presuppose a distinct vocation and a specific form of consecration, with a view to a particular mission.

For the mission of *the lay faithful*, whose proper task is to "seek the Kingdom of God by engaging in temporal affairs and by ordering them according to the plan of God,"[60] the consecration of Baptism and Confirmation common to all members of the People of God is a sufficient foundation. In addition to this basic consecration, *ordained ministers* receive the consecration of ordination in order to carry on the apostolic ministry in time. *Consecrated persons*, who embrace the evangelical counsels, receive a new and special consecration which, without being sacramental, commits them to making their own—in chastity, poverty, and obedience—the way of life practiced personally by Jesus and proposed by him to his disciples. Although these different categories are a manifestation of the one mystery of Christ, the lay faithful have as their specific but not exclusive characteristic, activity in the world; the clergy, ministry; consecrated men and women, special conformity to Christ, chaste, poor, and obedient.

The special value of the consecrated life

32. Within this harmonious constellation of gifts, each of the fundamental states of life is entrusted with the task of expressing, in its own way, one or other aspect of the one mystery of Christ. While *the lay life* has *a particular mission* of ensuring that the Gospel message is proclaimed in the temporal sphere, in the sphere of ecclesial communion *an indispensable ministry is carried out by those in Holy Orders*, and in a special way by bishops. The latter have the task of guiding the People of God by the teaching of the word, the administration of the sacraments, and the exercise of sacred power in the service of ecclesial communion, which is an organic communion, hierarchically structured.[61]

As a way of showing forth the Church's holiness, *it is to be recognized that the consecrated life*, which mirrors Christ's own way of life, *has an objective superiority*. Precisely for this reason, it is an especially rich manifestation of Gospel values and a more complete expression of the Church's purpose, which is the sanctification of humanity. The consecrated life proclaims and in a certain way anticipates the future age, when the fullness of the Kingdom of heaven, already present in its first fruits and in mystery,[62] will be achieved, and when the children of the resurrection will take neither wife nor husband, but will be like the angels of God (cf. Mt 22:30).

The Church has always taught the pre-eminence of perfect chastity for the sake of the Kingdom,[63] and rightly considers it the "door" of the whole consecrated life.[64] She also shows great esteem for the vocation to marriage, which makes spouses "witnesses to and cooperators in the fruitfulness of Holy Mother Church, who signify and share in the love with which Christ has loved his Bride and because of which he delivered himself up on her behalf."[65]

In this perspective, common to all consecrated life, there are many different but complementary paths. Men and women religious *completely devoted to contemplation* are in a special way an image of Christ praying on the mountain.[66] Consecrated persons engaged in *the active life* manifest Christ "in his proclamation of the Kingdom of God to the multitudes, in his healing of the sick and the suffering, in his work of converting sinners to a better life, in his solicitude for youth and his goodness to all."[67] Consecrated persons in *secular institutes* contribute in a special way to the coming of the Kingdom of God; they unite in a distinctive synthesis the value of consecration and that of being in the world. As they live their consecration in the world and from the world,[68] "they strive to imbue everything with an evangelical spirit for the strengthening and growth of the Body of Christ."[69] For this purpose they share in the Church's evangelizing mission through their personal witness of Christian living, their commitment to ordering temporal affairs according to God's plan, and their cooperation in service of the ecclesial community, in accordance with the secular way of life which is proper to them.[70]

Bearing witness to the Gospel of the Beatitudes

33. A particular duty of the consecrated life is to *remind the baptized of the fundamental values of the Gospel*, by bearing "splendid and striking testimony that the world cannot be transfigured and offered to God without the spirit of the Beatitudes."[71] The consecrated life thus continually fosters in the People of God an awareness of the need to respond with holiness of life to the love of God poured into their hearts by the Holy Spirit (cf. Rom 5:5), by reflecting in their conduct the sacramental consecration which is brought about by God's power in Baptism, Confirmation, or Holy Orders. In fact it is necessary to pass from the holiness communicated in the sacraments to the holiness of daily life. The consecrated life, by its very existence in the Church, seeks to serve the consecration of the lives of all the faithful, clergy and laity alike.

Nor must it be forgotten that consecrated persons themselves are helped by the witness of the other vocations to live fully and completely their union with the mystery of Christ and the Church in its many different dimensions. By virtue of this mutual enrichment, the mission of consecrated persons becomes more eloquent and effective: this mission is to remind their other brothers and sisters to keep their eyes fixed on the peace which is to come, and to strive for the definitive happiness found in God.

The living image of the Church as Bride

34. In the consecrated life, particular importance attaches to the spousal meaning, which recalls the Church's duty to be completely and exclusively devoted to her Spouse, from whom she receives every good thing. This spousal dimension, which is part of all consecrated life, has a particular meaning for women, who find therein their feminine identity and as it were discover the special genius of their relationship with the Lord.

A moving sign of this is seen in the New Testament passage which portrays Mary with the apostles in the upper room, in prayerful expectation of the Holy Spirit (cf. Acts 1:13–14). We can see here a vivid image of the Church as Bride, fully attentive to her Bridegroom and ready to accept his gift. In Peter and the other apostles there emerges above all the aspect of fruitfulness, as it is expressed in ecclesial ministry, which becomes an instrument of the Spirit for bringing new sons and daughters to birth through the preaching of the word, the celebration of the sacraments, and the giving of pastoral care. In Mary the aspect of spousal receptivity is particularly clear; it is under this aspect that the Church, through her perfect virginal life, brings divine life to fruition within herself.

The consecrated life has always been seen primarily in terms of Mary—Virgin and Bride. This virginal love is the source of a particular fruitfulness which fosters the birth and growth of divine life in people's hearts.[72] Following in the footsteps of Mary, the New Eve, consecrated persons express their spiritual fruitfulness by becoming receptive to the Word, in order to contribute to the growth of a new humanity by their unconditional dedication and their living witness. Thus the Church fully reveals her motherhood both in the communication of divine grace entrusted to Peter and in the responsible acceptance of God's gift, exemplified by Mary.

God's people, for their part, find in the ordained ministry the means of salvation, and in the consecrated life the incentive to make a full and loving response through all the different forms of Christian service.[73]

Ponder

This section offers a key to understanding what consecrated life *is* and the place it has in the Church. In fact, unless we see it in relation to the Church, it is impossible to understand what the consecrated life actually is.

For a long time, from the sixteenth century until Vatican II, the consecrated life was often seen primarily in terms of personal holiness, at least in the popular understanding. As a result, at times its reality as an ecclesial vocation was overshadowed.* Chastity, poverty, and obedience were seen as the privileged means of attaining holiness along a more narrow, more arduous way. And that pursuit of holiness was often seen as the main reason for people to enter the religious life.

This way of viewing consecrated life planted the seeds for the confusion that followed Vatican II. For the Council stressed that *all* the faithful are called to holiness; chapter 5 of *Lumen Gentium* develops this theme at length. So people thought that if *everyone* is called to holiness, and lay people can reach it just as much as religious can, then what's the point of dedicating one's life to pursuing holiness in a more arduous way? Why give up marriage and other goods? While the decline in vocations is a complex issue that has many

---

* See Consecrated Life in the *Ecclesiology of Vatican II*, by Janusz A. Ihnatowicz, S.T.D., http://www.ewtn.com/library/priests/fr91203.txt.

factors, the confusion about the call to holiness at least played a part.

How do we solve this dilemma? We need a change of perspective, one that sees the consecrated life not simply as a means to personal holiness, but as an *ecclesial* vocation that is absolutely essential for the life of the Church. John Paul II gives us the key for resolving the dilemma in this section of *Vita Consecrata*. He draws on the teaching of the Council, which in Chapter 6 of *Lumen Gentium* speaks of consecrated life in relation to the Church: "The evangelical counsels which lead to charity join their followers to the Church and its mystery in a special way" (no. 44). Here are the essential points that John Paul II makes:

A. Consecrated life is an essential element of the Church itself, for it expresses the very nature of the Church. It does this by making present the "way of life which Jesus himself chose and indicated as an absolute eschatological value" (no. 29).

B. This involves a new and special consecration that is rooted in Baptism and deepens the baptismal consecration. This consecration is a gift of the Holy Spirit that is given to some members of the Church.

C. The Holy Spirit gives a diversity of vocations, and there are three principal ones in the Church: to the lay life, to the ordained ministry, and to the consecrated life. Each of these vocations has its own gift and is essential to the Church. The laity live out their baptismal consecration by bringing the Kingdom of

God into the secular sphere; their vocation has a secular character. The ordained have the gift of ministry in the Church by teaching, shepherding, and administering the sacraments. The consecrated life is "a way of showing forth the Church's holiness . . . and a more complete expression of the Church's purpose, which is the sanctification of humanity" (no. 32). It also is a sign of the future age insofar as its members are configured to Christ, the chaste, poor, and obedient one, in a more radical way than others in the Church are called to live out.

Consecrated life does involve renunciation and is a way to holiness, but not in an individualistic sense. This way of holiness is pursued for the sake of the Church. As we will see in Chapter 3, it is a matter of a consecration for mission. This way of life is meant to show forth the Church's holiness by making Christ present. As John Paul II said earlier, Christ's radical way of living the Gospel is "the expression of his relationship as the only-begotten Son with the Father and with the Holy Spirit" (no. 18). So the consecrated life has the purpose of configuring us to Christ precisely in this way: Christ as the Son, living in union with the Father and the Holy Spirit. Christ thus draws people to live more profoundly the life of the Holy Trinity. That is what holiness is all about, and that is why the consecrated life is such an effective sign of the Church's holiness. It is truly a charism, a gift of the Spirit, that must always be present in the Church. Seeing consecrated life in this way can help us to understand why the universal call to holiness doesn't do away with the need for the consecrated life. In fact, consecrated life is meant to be an incentive to the other members of the Church to fully live their own vocations in holiness.

1. In number 34, John Paul II goes into more detail on the spousal meaning of the consecrated life. How does this add to the theological foundation he has already laid out in this chapter?

2. What is the difference between the roles of Peter and Mary in the Church, and how does that difference relate to the consecrated life?

Pray

Ask Mary to help you to live better your own vocation. You could talk to her informally, or pray the Hail Mary slowly a few times.

Act

This section of *Vita Consecrata* is dense and can be difficult to get through. Read it over a few times until you are clear about the line of thought John Paul II develops.

IV. Guided by the Spirit of Holiness

A "transfigured" life: the call to holiness

35. "When the disciples heard this, they fell on their faces, and were filled with fear" (Mt 17:6). In the episode of the transfiguration, the Synoptic Gospels, with varying nuances, point out the fear which overcomes the disciples. Their fascination at the transfigured face of Christ does not prevent them from being fearful before the divine Majesty which overshadows them. Whenever human beings become aware of the glory of God, they also become aware of their own insignificance and experience a sense of fear. Such fear is salutary. It reminds man of God's perfection, and at the same time urges him on with a pressing call to "holiness."

All the sons and daughters of the Church, called by God to "listen to" Christ, necessarily feel a *deep need for conversion and holiness*. But, as the Synod emphasized, this need in the first place challenges the consecrated life. In fact the vocation of consecrated persons to seek first the Kingdom of God is first and foremost a call to complete conversion, in self-renunciation, in order to live fully for the Lord, so that God may be all in all. Called to contemplate and bear witness to the transfigured face of Christ, consecrated men and women are also called to a "transfigured" existence.

The *Final Report* of the Second Extraordinary General Assembly of the Synod of Bishops made a significant observation in this regard: "Holy men and women have always been the source and origin of renewal in the most difficult circumstances throughout the Church's history. Today we have a tremendous need of saints, for whom we must assiduously implore God. The institutes of consecrated life, through the profession of the evangelical counsels, must be conscious of their special mission in today's Church, and we must encourage them in that mission."[74] The Fathers of the Ninth Assembly of the Synod of Bishops echoed this conviction: "Throughout the Church's history, consecrated life has been a living presence of the Spirit's work, a kind of privileged milieu for absolute love of God and of neighbor, for witness to the divine plan of gathering all humanity into the civilization of love, the great family of the children of God."[75]

The Church has always seen in the profession of the evangelical counsels a special path to holiness. The very expressions used to describe it—the school of the Lord's service, the school of love and holiness, the way or state of perfection—indicate the effectiveness and the wealth of means which are proper to this form of evangelical life, and the particular commitment made by those who embrace it.[76] It is not by chance that there have been so many consecrated persons down the centuries who have left behind eloquent testimonies of holiness and have undertaken particularly generous and demanding works of evangelization and service.

Faithfulness to the charism

36. In Christian discipleship and love for the person of Christ, there are a number of points concerning the growth of holiness in the consecrated life which merit particular emphasis today.

In the first place, there is the need for *fidelity to the founding charism* and subsequent spiritual heritage of each institute. It is precisely in this fidelity to the inspiration of the founders and foundresses, an inspiration which is itself a gift of the Holy Spirit, that the essential elements of the consecrated life can be more readily discerned and more fervently put into practice.

Fundamental to every charism is a threefold orientation. First, charisms lead *to the Father*, in the filial desire to seek his will through a process of unceasing conversion, wherein obedience is the source of true freedom, chastity expresses the yearning of a heart unsatisfied by any finite love, and poverty nourishes that hunger and thirst for justice which God has promised to satisfy (cf. Mt 5:6). Consequently the charism of each institute will lead the consecrated person to belong wholly to God, to speak with God or about God, as is said of Saint Dominic,[77] so that he or she can taste the goodness of the Lord (cf. Ps 34:8) in every situation.

Secondly, the charisms of the consecrated life also lead *to the Son*, fostering an intimate and joyful communion of life with him, in the school of his generous service of God and neighbor. Thus the attitude of consecrated persons "is progressively conformed to Christ; they learn detachment from externals, from the tumult of the senses, from all that keeps man from that freedom which allows him to be grasped by the Spirit."[78] As a result, consecrated persons are enabled to take up the mission of Christ, working and suffering with him in the spreading of his Kingdom.

Finally, every charism leads *to the Holy Spirit*, insofar as it prepares individuals to let themselves be guided and sustained by him, both in their personal spiritual journeys and in their lives of communion and apostolic work, in order to embody that attitude of service which should inspire the true Christian's every choice.

In fact it is this threefold relationship which emerges in every founding charism, though with the specific nuances of the various patterns of living. This is so because in every charism there predominates "a profound desire to be conformed to Christ to give witness to some aspect of his mystery."[79] This specific aspect is meant to take shape and develop according to the most authentic tradition of the institute, as present in its rule, constitutions, and statutes.[80]

Creative fidelity

37. Institutes of consecrated life are thus invited courageously to propose anew the enterprising initiative, creativity, and holiness of their founders and foundresses in response to the signs of the times emerging in today's world.[81] This invitation is first of all a call to perseverance on the path of holiness in the midst of the material and spiritual difficulties of daily life. But it is also a call to pursue competence in personal work and to develop a dynamic fidelity to their mission, adapting forms, if need be, to new situations and different needs, in complete openness to God's inspiration and to the Church's discernment. But all must be fully convinced that the quest for ever greater conformity to the Lord is the guarantee of any

renewal which seeks to remain faithful to an institute's original inspiration.[82]

In this spirit there is a pressing need today for every institute *to return to the rule*, since the rule and constitutions provide a map for the whole journey of discipleship, in accordance with a specific charism confirmed by the Church. A greater regard for the rule will not fail to offer consecrated persons a reliable criterion in their search for the appropriate forms of a witness which is capable of responding to the needs of the times without departing from an institute's initial inspiration.

Prayer and asceticism: spiritual combat

38. The call to holiness is accepted and can be cultivated only *in the silence of adoration* before the infinite transcendence of God: "We must confess that we all have need of this silence, filled with the presence of him who is adored: in theology, so as to exploit fully its own sapiential and spiritual soul; in prayer, so that we may never forget that seeing God means coming down the mountain with a face so radiant that we are obliged to cover it with a veil (cf. Ex 34:33); in commitment, so that we will refuse to be locked in a struggle without love and forgiveness. All, believers and non-believers alike, need to learn a silence that allows the Other to speak when and how he wishes, and allows us to understand his words."[83] In practice this involves great fidelity to liturgical and personal prayer, to periods devoted to mental prayer and contemplation, to Eucharistic adoration, to monthly retreats, and to spiritual exercises.

There is also a need to rediscover the *ascetic practices* typical of the spiritual tradition of the Church and of the individual's own institute. These have been and continue to be a powerful aid to authentic progress in holiness. Asceticism, by helping to master and correct the inclinations of human nature wounded by sin, is truly indispensable if consecrated persons are to remain faithful to their own vocation and follow Jesus on the way of the cross.

It is also necessary to recognize and overcome certain temptations which sometimes, by diabolical deceit, present themselves under the appearance of good. Thus, for example, the legitimate need to be familiar with today's society in order to respond to its challenges can lead to a surrender to passing fashions with a consequent lessening of spiritual fervor or a succumbing to discouragement. The possibility of a deeper spiritual formation might lead consecrated persons to feel somehow superior to other members of the faithful, while the urgent need for appropriate and necessary training can turn into a frantic quest for efficiency, as if apostolic service depended primarily on human means rather than on God. The praiseworthy desire to become close to the men and women of our day, believers and non-believers, rich and poor, can lead to the adoption of a secularized lifestyle or the promotion of human values in a merely horizontal direction. Sharing in the legitimate aspirations of one's own nation or culture could lead to embracing forms of nationalism or accepting customs which instead need to be purified and elevated in the light of the Gospel.

The path to holiness thus involves *the acceptance of spiritual combat*. This is a demanding reality which is not always given due attention today. Tradition has often seen an image of this spiritual combat in Jacob's wrestling with the mystery of God, whom he confronts in order to receive his blessing and to see him (cf. Gen 32:23–31). In this episode from the beginnings of biblical history, consecrated persons can recognize a symbol of the asceticism which they need in order to open their hearts to the Lord and to their brothers and sisters.

Fostering holiness

39. Today a renewed commitment to holiness by consecrated persons is more necessary than ever, also as *a means of promoting and supporting every Christian's desire for perfection.* "It is therefore necessary to inspire in all the faithful a true longing for holiness, a deep desire for conversion and personal renewal in a context of ever more intense prayer and of solidarity with one's neighbor, especially the most needy."[84]

To the degree that they deepen their friendship with God, consecrated persons become better prepared to help their brothers and sisters through valuable spiritual activities such as schools of prayer, spiritual exercises and retreats, days of recollection, spiritual dialogue and direction. In this way people are helped to grow in prayer and will then be better able to discern God's will in their lives and to commit themselves to the courageous and sometimes heroic demands which faith makes of them. Consecrated persons "at the deepest level of their being . . . are caught up in the dynamism of the Church's life, which is thirsty for the divine Absolute and called to holiness. It is to this holiness that they bear witness,"[85] The fact that all are called to become saints cannot fail to inspire more and more those who by their very choice of life have the mission of reminding others of that call.

"Rise, and have no fear": a renewed trust

40. "Jesus came and touched them, saying, 'Rise, and have no fear'" (Mt 17:7). Like the three apostles in the episode of the transfiguration, consecrated persons know from experience that their lives are not always marked by the fervor which makes us exclaim: "It is well that we are here" (Mt 17:4). But it is always a life "touched" by the hand of Christ, a life where his voice is heard, a life sustained by his grace.

"Rise, and have no fear." Obviously, the Master's encouragement is addressed to every Christian. All the more does it apply to those called to "leave everything" and thus to "risk everything" for Christ. This is particularly true whenever one descends from the "mountain" with the Master and sets off on the road which leads from Tabor to Calvary.

When Luke relates that Moses and Elijah were speaking with Christ about his Paschal Mystery, it is significant that he uses the term "departure" (*éxodos*): "they spoke about his departure, which he was to accomplish at Jerusalem" (9:31). "Exodus" is a basic term in revelation; it evokes the whole of salvation history and expresses the deep meaning of the Paschal Mystery. It is a theme particularly dear to the spirituality of the consecrated life and well expresses its meaning. It inevitably includes everything that pertains to the *mysterium crucis*. But this difficult "exodus journey," when viewed from the perspective of Tabor, is seen to be a road situated between two lights: the anticipatory light of the transfiguration and the definitive light of the resurrection.

From the standpoint of the Christian life as a whole, the vocation to the consecrated life is, despite its renunciations and trials, and indeed because of them, *a path "of light"* over which the Redeemer keeps constant watch: *"Rise, and have no fear."*

Ponder

"Today we have a tremendous need of saints" (no. 35). John Paul II focuses on the need for holiness and prayer, seeing the spiritual journey as being situated between two points of light: the transfiguration and the resurrection. Encouraged by our mountain-top experiences with Jesus, we find the courage we need to keep on going when the cross enters our lives. Ongoing conversion and self-renunciation are essential for spiritual growth. John Paul II situates this growth in terms of our relationship with the Trinity. He says that faithfulness to one's charism leads first of all to the Father. The vows of poverty, chastity, and obedience help the consecrated person to give up selfish desires so as to belong wholly to God. Union with the Son leads to taking up his mission to bring others into the Kingdom. The Holy Spirit guides and sustains us in this work.

John Paul II was realistic about human nature, recognizing that over time we can grow weary on the spiritual journey. Our "lives are not always marked by the fervor which makes us exclaim, 'It is well that we are here'" (no. 40). The Catholic spiritual tradition has spoken of this in terms of sloth, or better, *acedia*, which is a kind of sorrow over spiritual good because it is an arduous good. Acedia strikes at love, because as Saint Thomas says, it "belongs especially to charity to have that spiritual joy whereby one rejoices in the Divine good."[*]

---

[*] *Summa Theol.*, II–II, q. 35, a. 2.

Anyone who has spent any time in the consecrated life knows that spiritual weariness will eventually crop up and may bring the temptation to give up the struggle. But John Paul II encourages us to continue, reminding us that "the path to holiness thus involves *the acceptance of spiritual combat*" (no. 38).

The idea of the spiritual life as a battle can be found in Saint Paul and may appeal especially to men. "Therefore take up the whole armor of God, so that you may be able to withstand on that evil day. . . . Take the helmet of salvation, and the sword of the Spirit, which is the word of God" (Eph 6:13, 17). This is not a battle against other people, but against our own inclinations to sin and weakness. In the spiritual struggle the support of others in community can help us immensely. In a talk I once heard about spirituality for men, the speaker used the image of the "band of brothers" who always have each other's backs. Women may have other ways of supporting each other in community, but the important thing is to have concern for those who may be going through difficult times.

Living a holy life means not only avoiding sin but also being rooted in the virtues. John Paul II recalls some basics, stressing the need not only for prayer but also for a wise asceticism, which helps "to master and correct the inclinations of human nature wounded by sin" (no. 38). The cardinal virtue of temperance helps us to regulate our desires, especially in regard to sexuality and food. But we can easily go overboard in any area of life, depending on our personal needs and wants. The purpose of asceticism is to free us from being controlled by our own inordinate desires. Such freedom will benefit not only those in consecrated life, but also the persons they are called to serve. All are called to holiness, and consecrated persons will be better able to help others hear and respond to that call to the degree that they themselves respond to it. This builds up the whole Church in love.

1. If you find yourself getting weary on the spiritual journey, what can you do to recover a sense of enthusiasm and joy? If you have gone through weariness in the past, how did you get over it?

2. Is there some area in your life where you can achieve greater interior freedom through self-discipline? What would your life look like if you did this?

3. How do you see your life of prayer and union with God as connected to the spiritual well-being of others? In what ways might you be able to help others grow in their own spiritual journey?

Pray

In number 38 the Pope lists some specific forms of prayer: liturgical and personal prayer, mental prayer and contemplation, Eucharistic adoration, monthly retreats and spiritual exercises. If you are already doing any of these, pick one that may have become routine and do it more intentionally, with greater awareness and love.

Act

The following thoughts on penance are from Blessed James Alberione, the founder of the Pauline Family. Is there some specific area in your life where you can move forward by developing your gifts? What might that be, and in what way could you do so?

Three penances are included in our constitutions. The first is common to all religious: common life lived with love, constantly, joyously.

The second is the predominant one: the development of one's personality, to progress more and more, to develop one's gifts and talents of both nature and grace. To ever better apply one's mind in the things of God and the service of the mission. To be increasingly skilled and industrious in one's responsibilities, and more and more fervent in the practice of prayer and religious observance.

The third is to apply, use, and bring together everything for the glory of God, the mission, to merit for heaven. Always forward, always progress, always prepare for the heavenly life that awaits us. . . . Our penances are not to weaken or to drain us, nor to harm our health, our gifts, the energies of mind, heart, body . . . They are instead an ongoing study of how to use everything for God, souls, holiness.

(*San Paolo*, Internal Bulletin of the Society of St. Paul, Rome, April 1949)

Chapter II

Signum Fraternitatis
Consecrated Life as a Sign of Communion in the Church

I. Permanent Values

In the image of the Trinity

41. During his earthly life, the Lord Jesus called those whom he wished in order to have them at his side and to train them to live, according to his example, for the Father and for the mission which he had received from the Father (cf. Mk 3:13–15). He thus inaugurated the new family which down the centuries would include all those ready to "do the will of God" (cf. Mk 3:32–35). After the ascension, as a result of the gift of the Spirit, a fraternal community formed around the apostles, gathered in the praise of God and in a concrete experience of communion (cf. Acts 2:42–47; 4:32–35). The life of that community and, even more, the experience of complete sharing with Christ lived out by the Twelve, have always been the *model to which the Church has looked* whenever she has

sought to return to her original fervor and to resume with fresh evangelical vigor her journey through history.[86]

The Church is essentially a mystery of communion, "a people made one with the unity of the Father, the Son, and the Holy Spirit."[87] The fraternal life seeks to reflect the depth and richness of this mystery, taking shape as a human community in which the Trinity dwells, in order to extend in history the gifts of communion proper to the three divine Persons. Many are the settings and the ways in which fraternal communion is expressed in the life of the Church. The consecrated life can certainly be credited with having effectively helped to keep alive in the Church the obligation of fraternity as a form of witness to the Trinity. By constantly promoting fraternal love, also in the form of common life, the consecrated life has shown that *sharing in the Trinitarian communion can change human relationships* and create a new type of solidarity. In this way it speaks to people both of the beauty of fraternal communion and of the ways which actually lead to it. Consecrated persons live "for" God and "from" God, and precisely for this reason they are able to bear witness to the reconciling power of grace, which overcomes the divisive tendencies present in the human heart and in society.

Fraternal life in love

42. The fraternal life, understood as a life shared in love, is an eloquent sign of ecclesial communion. It is practiced with special care in religious institutes and in societies of apostolic life, where community living acquires special significance.[88] Nor is the dimension of fraternal communion alien to secular

institutes, or even to forms of the consecrated life lived individually. Hermits, in their profound solitude, do not withdraw from ecclesial communion but serve that communion by their specific charism of contemplation. Consecrated virgins in the world live out their consecration in a special relationship of communion with the particular and universal Church. The same is true of consecrated widows and widowers.

All these people, by practicing evangelical discipleship, commit themselves to fulfilling the Lord's "new commandment," to love one another as he has loved us (cf. Jn 13:34). Love led Christ to the gift of self, even to the supreme sacrifice of the cross. So too, among his disciples, *there can be no true unity without that unconditional mutual love* which demands a readiness to serve others generously, a willingness to welcome them as they are, without "judging" them (cf. Mt 7:1–2), and an ability to forgive up to "seventy times seven" (Mt 18:22). Consecrated persons, who become "of one heart and soul" (Acts 4:32) through the love poured into their hearts by the Holy Spirit (cf. Rom 5:5), experience an interior call *to share everything in common*: material goods and spiritual experiences, talents and inspirations, apostolic ideals and charitable service: "In community life, the power of the Holy Spirit at work in one individual passes at the same time to all. Here not only does each enjoy his own gift, but makes it abound by sharing it with others; and each one enjoys the fruits of the other's gift as if they were his own."[89]

In community life, then, it should in some way be evident that, more than an instrument for carrying out a specific mission, fraternal communion is *a God-enlightened space* in which to experience the hidden presence of the Risen Lord (cf. Mt 18:20).[90] This comes about through the mutual love of all the members of the community, a love nourished by the word and by the Eucharist, purified in the Sacrament of Reconciliation, and sustained by prayer for unity, the special gift of the Spirit to those who obediently listen to the Gospel. It is the Spirit himself who leads the soul to the experience of communion with the Father and with his Son Jesus Christ (cf. 1 Jn 1:3), a communion which is the source of fraternal life. It is the Spirit who guides communities of the consecrated life in carrying out their mission of service to the Church and to all humanity, in accordance with their original inspiration.

In this perspective, special importance attaches to chapters (or similar meetings), whether particular or general, at which institutes are called to elect superiors according to the norms set out in their constitutions, and to discern, in the light of the Spirit, the best ways to preserve and adapt their charism and their spiritual patrimony to changing historical and cultural situations.[91]

The task of authority

43. In the consecrated life the role of superiors, including local superiors, has always been of great importance for the spiritual life and for mission. In these years of change and experimentation, the need to revise this office has sometimes been felt. But it should be recognized that those who exercise authority *cannot renounce their obligation as those first responsible* for the community, as guides of their brothers and sisters in the spiritual and apostolic life.

In an atmosphere strongly affected by individualism, it is not an easy thing to foster recognition and acceptance of the role which authority plays for the benefit of all. Nevertheless, its importance must be reaffirmed as essential for strengthening fraternal communion and in order not to render vain the obedience professed. While authority must be above all fraternal and spiritual, and while those entrusted with it must know how to involve their brothers and sisters in the decision-making process, it should still be remembered that *the final word belongs to authority* and, consequently, that authority has the right to see that decisions taken are respected.[92]

The role of the elderly

44. Caring for the elderly and the sick has an important place in the fraternal life, especially at times like the present, when in some parts of the world the percentage of elderly consecrated persons is increasing. The care and concern which these persons deserve arises not only from a clear obligation of charity and gratitude but also from an awareness that their witness greatly serves the Church and their own institutes, and that their mission continues to be worthwhile and meritorious, even when for reasons of age or infirmity they have had to abandon their specific apostolate. *The elderly and the sick have a great deal to give* in wisdom and experience to the community, if only the community can remain close to them with concern and an ability to listen.

More than in any activity, the apostolate consists in the witness of one's own complete dedication to the Lord's saving will, a dedication nourished by the practice of prayer and of penance. The elderly are called in many ways to live out their vocation: by persevering prayer, by patient acceptance of their condition, and by their readiness to serve as spiritual directors, confessors, or mentors in prayer.[93]

In the image of the apostolic community

45. The fraternal life plays a fundamental role in the spiritual journey of consecrated persons, both for their constant renewal and for the full accomplishment of their mission in the world. This is evident from the theological motivations which sustain it, and is amply confirmed by experience. I therefore exhort consecrated men and women to commit themselves to strengthening their fraternal life, following the example of the first Christians in Jerusalem who were assiduous in accepting the teaching of the apostles, in common prayer, in celebrating the Eucharist, and in sharing whatever goods of nature and grace they had (cf. Acts 2:42–47). Above all I call upon men and women religious and members of societies of apostolic life to show generous mutual love, expressing it in ways which are in keeping with the nature of each institute, so that every community will be revealed as a luminous sign of the new Jerusalem, "the dwelling of God with men" (Rev 21:3).

The whole Church greatly depends on the witness of communities filled "with joy and with the Holy Spirit" (Acts 13:52). She wishes to hold up before the world the example of communities in which solitude is overcome through concern for one another, in which communication inspires in everyone a sense of shared responsibility, and in which wounds are healed through forgiveness, and each person's commitment to communion is strengthened. The nature of the charism in communities of this kind directs their energies, sustains their fidelity, and directs the apostolic work of all toward the one mission. If the Church is to reveal her true face to today's world, she urgently needs such fraternal communities, which, by their very existence, contribute to the new evangelization, inasmuch as they disclose in a concrete way the fruitfulness of the "new commandment."

"Sentire cum Ecclesia"

46. A great task also belongs to the consecrated life in the light of the teaching about the Church as communion so strongly proposed by the Second Vatican Council. Consecrated persons are asked to be true experts of communion and to practice the spirituality of communion[94] as "witnesses and architects of the plan for unity which is the crowning point of human history in God's design."[95] The sense of ecclesial communion, developing into a *spirituality of communion*, promotes a way of thinking, speaking, and acting which enables the Church to grow in depth and extension. The life of communion in fact "becomes a *sign* for all the world and a compelling *force* that leads people to faith in Christ. . . . In this way communion leads to *mission*, and itself becomes mission"; indeed, *"communion begets communion: in essence it is a communion that is missionary."*[96]

In founders and foundresses *we see a constant and lively sense of the Church*, which they manifest by their full participation in all aspects of the Church's life, and in their ready obedience to the bishops and especially to the Roman Pontiff. Against this background of love toward Holy Church, "the pillar and bulwark of the truth" (1 Tim 3:15), we readily understand the devotion of Saint Francis of Assisi for "the Lord Pope,"[97] the daughterly outspokenness of Saint Catherine of Siena toward the one whom she called "sweet Christ on earth,"[98] the apostolic obedience and the *sentire cum Ecclesia* of Saint Ignatius Loyola,[99] and the joyful profession of faith made by Saint Teresa of Avila: "I am a daughter of the Church."[100] We can also understand the deep desire of Saint Theresa of the Child Jesus: "In the heart of the Church, my mother, I will be love."[101] These testimonies are representative of the full ecclesial communion which the saints, founders and foundresses, have shared in diverse and often difficult times and circumstances. They are examples which consecrated persons need constantly to recall if they are to resist the particularly strong centrifugal and disruptive forces at work today.

A distinctive aspect of ecclesial communion is allegiance of mind and heart to the Magisterium of the bishops, an allegiance which must be lived honestly, and clearly testified to before the People of God by all consecrated persons, especially those involved in theological research, teaching, publishing, catechesis, and the use of the means of social communication.[102] Because consecrated persons have a special place in the Church, their attitude in this regard is of immense importance for the whole People of God. Their witness of filial love will give power and forcefulness to their apostolic activity which, in the context of the prophetic mission of all the

baptized, is generally distinguished by special forms of cooperation with the hierarchy.[103] In a specific way, through the
richness of their charisms, consecrated persons help the
Church to reveal ever more deeply her nature as the sacrament
"of intimate union with God, and of the unity of all
mankind."[104]

Fraternity in the universal Church

47. Consecrated persons are called to be a leaven of communion at the service of the mission of the universal Church
by the very fact that the manifold charisms of their respective
institutes are granted by the Holy Spirit for the good of the
entire Mystical Body, whose upbuilding they must serve (cf. 1
Cor 12:4–11). Significantly, "the more excellent way" (1 Cor
12:31), the "greatest of all" (cf. 1 Cor 13:13), as the Apostle
says, is charity, which brings all diversity into one and strengthens everyone to support one another in apostolic zeal. This,
precisely, is the scope of *the particular bond of communion* which
the different institutes of consecrated life and the societies of
apostolic life *have with the Successor of Peter in his ministry of
unity and missionary universality*. The history of spirituality
amply illustrates this bond and shows its providential function
both in safeguarding the specific identity of the consecrated
life and in advancing the missionary expansion of the Gospel.
The vigorous spread of the Gospel message, the firm rooting
of the Church in so many areas of the world, and the Christian
springtime which the young Churches are experiencing today,
would be unthinkable—as the Synod Fathers observed—
without the contribution of numerous institutes of consecrated

life and societies of apostolic life. Down the centuries they have maintained strong bonds of communion with the Successors of Peter, who found in them a generous readiness to devote themselves to the Church's missionary activity with an availability which, when necessary, went as far as heroism.

All this brings out *the character of universality and communion* proper to institutes of consecrated life and to societies of apostolic life. Because of their supra-diocesan character, grounded in their special relation to the Petrine ministry, they are also at the service of cooperation among the particular Churches,[105] since they can effectively promote an "exchange of gifts" among them, and thus contribute to an inculturation of the Gospel which purifies, strengthens and ennobles the treasures found in the cultures of all peoples.[106] Today too, the flowering of vocations to the consecrated life in the younger Churches demonstrates the ability of the consecrated life to make present in Catholic unity the needs of different peoples and cultures.

The consecrated life and the particular Church

48. Again, a significant role is played by consecrated persons *within the particular Churches*. On the basis of the Council's teaching on the Church as communion and mystery, and on the particular Churches as portions of the People of God in which "the one, holy, catholic, and apostolic Church of Christ is truly present and operative,"[107] this aspect of the consecrated life has been systematically explored and codified in various postconciliar documents. These texts bring out clearly the fundamental importance of cooperation between

consecrated persons and bishops for the organic development of diocesan pastoral life. The charisms of the consecrated life can greatly contribute to the building up of charity in the particular Churches.

The various ways of living the evangelical counsels are in fact the expression and fruit of spiritual gifts received by founders and foundresses. As such, they constitute an "*experience of the Spirit,* transmitted to their disciples to be lived, safeguarded, deepened, and constantly developed by them, in harmony with the Body of Christ continually in the process of growth."[108] The identity of each institute is bound up with a particular spirituality and apostolate, which takes shape in a specific tradition marked by objective elements.[109] For this reason the Church is concerned that institutes should grow and develop in accordance with the spirit of their founders and foundresses and their own sound traditions.[110]

Consequently, each institute is recognized as having *a rightful autonomy,* enabling it to follow its own discipline and to keep intact its spiritual and apostolic patrimony. It is the responsibility of local Ordinaries to preserve and safeguard this autonomy.[111] Thus, bishops are asked to welcome and esteem the charisms of the consecrated life, and to give them a place in the pastoral plans of the diocese. They should have a particular concern for institutes of diocesan right, which are entrusted to the special care of the local bishop. A diocese which lacked the consecrated life would not only be deprived of many spiritual gifts, of suitable places for people to seek God, of specific apostolic activities and pastoral approaches, but it would also risk a great weakening of that missionary spirit which is characteristic of the majority of institutes.[112] There is a duty then to respond to the gift of the consecrated life, which the Spirit awakens in the particular Churches, by welcoming it with generosity and thanksgiving.

Fruitful and ordered ecclesial communion

49. The bishop is the father and pastor of the particular Church in its entirety. It is his task to discern and respect individual charisms, and to promote and coordinate them. In his pastoral charity he will therefore welcome the charism of the consecrated life as a grace which is not restricted to any one institute, but which benefits the whole Church. Bishops will thus seek to support and help consecrated persons, so that, in communion with the Church, they open themselves to spiritual and pastoral initiatives responding to the needs of our time, while remaining faithful to their founding charism. For their part, consecrated persons will not fail to cooperate generously with the particular Churches as much as they can and with respect for their own charism, *working in full communion with the bishop* in the areas of evangelization, catechesis, and parish life.

It is helpful to recall that, in coordinating their service to the universal Church with their service to the particular Churches, institutes may not invoke rightful autonomy, or even the exemption which a number of them enjoy,[113] in order to justify choices which actually conflict with the demands of organic communion called for by a healthy ecclesial life. Instead, the pastoral initiatives of consecrated persons should be determined and carried out in cordial and open dialogue between bishops and superiors of the different institutes. Special attention by bishops to the vocation and mission of institutes, and respect by the latter for the ministry of bishops, with ready acceptance of their concrete pastoral directives for the life of the diocese: these are two intimately linked expressions of that one ecclesial charity by which all work to build up the organic communion—charismatic and at the same time hierarchically structured of the whole People of God.

A constant dialogue animated by charity

50. *Constant dialogue* between superiors of institutes of consecrated life and societies of apostolic life and bishops is most valuable in order to promote mutual understanding, which is the necessary precondition for effective cooperation, especially in pastoral matters. Thanks to regular contacts of this kind, superiors, both men and women, can inform bishops about the apostolic undertakings which they are planning in dioceses, in order to agree on the necessary practical arrangements. In the same way, it is helpful for delegates of the conferences of major superiors to be invited to meetings of the bishops' conferences and, in turn, for delegates of the episcopal conferences to be invited to attend the conferences of major superiors, following predetermined formats. It would be a great help if, where they do not yet exist, *mixed commissions of bishops and major superiors*[114] were set up at the national level for the joint study of problems of common interest. Likewise, better reciprocal knowledge will result if the theology and the spirituality of the consecrated life are made part

of the theological preparation of diocesan priests, and if adequate attention to the theology of the particular Church and to the spirituality of the diocesan clergy is included in the formation of consecrated persons.[115]

Finally, it is reassuring to mention that, at the Synod, not only were there many interventions on the doctrine of communion, but great satisfaction was expressed for the experience of dialogue conducted in a climate of mutual trust and openness between the bishops and the men and women religious present. This led to a desire that "this spiritual experience of communion and cooperation be extended to the whole Church," even after the Synod.[116] It is my hope too that all will grow in the understanding and spirituality of communion.

Fraternity in a divided and unjust world

51. The Church entrusts to communities of consecrated life the particular task of *spreading the spirituality of communion*, first of all in their internal life and then in the ecclesial community, and even beyond its boundaries, by opening or continuing a dialogue in charity, especially where today's world is torn apart by ethnic hatred or senseless violence. Placed as they are within the world's different societies—societies frequently marked by conflicting passions and interests, seeking unity but uncertain about the ways to attain it—communities of consecrated life, where persons of different ages, languages, and cultures meet as brothers and sisters, are *signs that dialogue is always possible* and that communion can bring differences into harmony.

Consecrated men and women are sent forth to proclaim, by the witness of their lives, the value of Christian fraternity and the transforming power of the Good News,[117] which makes it possible to see all people as sons and daughters of God, and inspires a self-giving love toward everyone, especially the least of our brothers and sisters. Such communities are places of hope and of the discovery of the Beatitudes, where love, drawing strength from prayer, the wellspring of communion, is called to become a pattern of life and source of joy.

In an age characterized by the globalization of problems and the return of the idols of nationalism, international institutes especially are called to uphold and to bear witness to the sense of communion between peoples, races, and cultures. In a climate of fraternity, an openness to the global dimension of problems will not detract from the richness of particular gifts, nor will the affirmation of a particular gift conflict with other gifts or with unity itself. International institutes can achieve this effectively, inasmuch as they have to face in a creative way the challenge of inculturation, while at the same time preserving their identity.

Communion among different institutes

52. Fraternal spiritual relations and mutual cooperation among different institutes of consecrated life and societies of apostolic life are sustained and nourished by the sense of ecclesial communion. Those who are united by a common commitment to the following of Christ and are inspired by the same Spirit cannot fail to manifest visibly, as branches of

the one vine, the fullness of the Gospel of love. Mindful of the spiritual friendship which often united founders and found-resses during their lives, consecrated persons, while remaining faithful to the character of their own institute, are called to practice a fraternity which is exemplary and which will serve to encourage the other members of the Church in the daily task of bearing witness to the Gospel.

Saint Bernard's words about the various religious orders remain ever timely: "I admire them all. I belong to one of them by observance, but to all of them by charity. We all need one another: the spiritual good which I do not own and pos-sess, I receive from others . . . in this exile, the Church is still on pilgrimage and is, in a certain sense, plural: she is a single plurality and a plural unity. All our diversities, which make manifest the richness of God's gifts, will continue to exist in the one house of the Father, which has many rooms. Now there is a division of graces; then there will be distinctions of glory. Unity, both here and there, consists in one and the same charity."[118]

Coordinating bodies

53. A significant contribution to communion can be made by the conferences of major superiors and by the conferences of secular institutes. Encouraged and regulated by the Second Vatican Council[119] and by subsequent documents[120] these bodies have as their principal purpose the promotion of the consecrated life within the framework of the Church's mission.

By means of these bodies, institutes express the communion which unites them, and they seek the means to reinforce that communion, with respect and esteem for the uniqueness of their different charisms, which reflect the mystery of the Church and the richness of divine wisdom.[121] I encourage institutes of consecrated life to work together, especially in those countries where particularly difficult situations increase the temptation for them to withdraw into themselves, to the detriment of the consecrated life itself and of the Church. Rather, these institutes should help one another in trying to *discern God's plan* in this troubled moment of history, in order better to respond to it with appropriate works of the apostolate.[122] In the perspective of a communion open to the challenges of our time, superiors, men and women, "working in harmony with the bishops," should seek "to make use of the accomplishments of the best members of each institute and to offer services which not only help to overcome eventual limits but which create a valid style of formation in consecrated life."[123]

I exhort the conferences of major superiors and the conferences of secular institutes to maintain frequent and regular contacts with the Congregation for Institutes of Consecrated Life and Societies of Apostolic Life, as a sign of their communion with the Holy See. An active and trusting relationship ought also to be maintained with the episcopal conference of each country. In the spirit of the document *Mutuae Relationes*, these contacts should be established on a stable basis, in order to provide for constant and timely coordination of initiatives as they come up. If all this is done with perseverance and a spirit of faithful adherence to the directives of the Magisterium, the organizations which promote coordination and communion will prove to be particularly helpful in formulating solutions which avoid misunderstandings and tensions both on the theoretical and practical levels.[124] In this way they will make a positive contribution not only to the growth of communion between institutes of consecrated life and the bishops, but also to the advancement of the mission of the particular Churches.

Communion and cooperation with the laity

54. In recent years, one of the fruits of the teaching on the Church as communion has been the growing awareness that her members can and must unite their efforts, with a view to cooperation and exchange of gifts, in order to participate more effectively in the Church's mission. This helps to give a clearer and more complete picture of the Church herself, while rendering more effective the response to the great challenges of our time, thanks to the combined contributions of the various gifts.

Contacts with the laity, in the case of monastic or contemplative institutes, take the form of a relationship that is primarily spiritual, while for institutes involved in works of the apostolate these contacts also translate into forms of pastoral cooperation. Members of secular institutes, lay or clerical, relate to other members of the faithful at the level of everyday life. Today, often as a result of new situations, many institutes have come to the conclusion that *their charism can be shared with the laity.* The laity are therefore invited to share more intensely in the spirituality and mission of these institutes. We may say that, in the light of certain historical experiences such as those of the secular or third orders, a new chapter, rich in hope, has begun in the history of relations between consecrated persons and the laity.

For a renewed spiritual and apostolic dynamism

55. These new experiences of communion and cooperation should be encouraged for various reasons. They can in fact give rise to the spread of a fruitful spirituality beyond the confines of the institute, which will then be in a position to ensure the continuity in the Church of the services typical of the institute. Another positive consequence will be to facilitate more intense cooperation between consecrated persons and the laity in view of the institute's mission. Moved by the examples of holiness of the consecrated members, lay men and women will experience at first hand the spirit of the evangelical counsels, and will thus be encouraged to live and bear witness to the spirit of the Beatitudes, in order to transform the world according to God's design.[125]

The participation of the laity often brings unexpected and rich insights into certain aspects of the charism, leading to a more spiritual interpretation of it and helping to draw from it directions for new activities in the apostolate. In whatever activity or ministry they are involved, consecrated persons should remember that before all else they must be expert guides in the spiritual life, and in this perspective they should cultivate "the most precious gift: the spirit."[126] For their part, the laity should offer religious families the invaluable contribution of their "being in the world" and their specific service.

Associates and lay volunteers

56. A significant expression of lay people's sharing in the richness of the consecrated life is their participation in various institutes under the new form of so-called associate members or, in response to conditions present in certain cultures, as people who share fully for a certain period of time the institute's community life and its particular dedication to contemplation or the apostolate. This should always be done in such a way that the identity of the institute in its internal life is not harmed.[127]

This voluntary service, which draws from the richness of the consecrated life, should be held in great esteem; it is however necessary to provide proper formation so that, besides being competent, volunteers always have supernaturally motivated intentions and, in their projects, a strong sense of community and of the Church.[128] Moreover, it should be borne in mind that initiatives involving lay persons at the decision-making level, in order to be considered the work of a specific institute, must promote the ends of that institute and be carried out under its responsibility. Therefore, if lay persons take on a directive role, they will be accountable for their actions to the competent superiors. It is necessary for all this to be examined and regulated by special directives in each institute, to be approved by higher authority; these directives should indicate the respective responsibilities of the institute itself, of its communities, associate members, and volunteers.

Consecrated persons, sent by their superiors and remaining subject to them, can take part in *specific forms of cooperation in lay initiatives*, particularly in organizations and institutions which work with those on the margins of society and which have the purpose of alleviating human suffering. Such collaboration, if prompted and sustained by a clear and strong Christian identity and respectful of the particular character of the consecrated life, can make the radiant power of the Gospel shine forth brightly even in the darkest situations of human life.

In recent years, many consecrated persons have become members of one or other of the *ecclesial movements* which have spread in our time. From these experiences, those involved usually draw benefit, especially in the area of spiritual renewal. Nonetheless, it cannot be denied that in certain cases this involvement causes uneasiness and disorientation at the personal or community level, especially when these experiences come into conflict with the demands of the common life or of the institute's spirituality. It is therefore necessary to take care that membership in these ecclesial movements does not endanger the charism or discipline of the institute of origin,[129] and that all is done with the permission of superiors and with the full intention of accepting their decisions.

The dignity and role of consecrated women

57. The Church fully reveals her varied spiritual richness when she overcomes all discrimination and welcomes as a true blessing the gifts lavished by God upon both men and women, considering them in their equal dignity. By virtue of

their dedication lived in fullness and in joy, consecrated women are called in a very special way to be *signs of God's tender love toward the human race* and to be special witnesses to the mystery of the Church, Virgin, Bride, and Mother.[130] This mission of theirs was noted by the Synod, in which many consecrated women participated and made their voices heard. Those voices were listened to and appreciated. Thanks also to their contribution, useful directions for the Church's life and her evangelizing mission have emerged. Certainly, the validity of many assertions relating to the position of women in different sectors of society and of the Church cannot be denied. It is equally important to point out that women's new self-awareness also helps men to reconsider their way of looking at things, the way they understand themselves, where they place themselves in history and how they interpret it, and the way they organize social, political, economic, religious, and ecclesial life.

Having received from Christ a message of liberation, the Church has the mission to proclaim this message prophetically, promoting ways of thinking and acting which correspond to the mind of the Lord. In this context the consecrated woman, on the basis of her experience of the Church and as a woman in the Church, can help eliminate certain one-sided perspectives which do not fully recognize her dignity and her specific contribution to the Church's life and pastoral and missionary activity. Consecrated women therefore rightly aspire to have their identity, ability, mission, and responsibility more clearly recognized, both in the awareness of the Church and in everyday life.

Likewise, the future of the new evangelization, as of all other forms of missionary activity, is unthinkable without a renewed contribution from women, especially consecrated women.

New possibilities of presence and action

58. It is therefore urgently necessary to take certain concrete steps, beginning by *providing room for women to participate* in different fields and at all levels, including decision-making processes, above all in matters which concern women themselves.

Moreover, the formation of consecrated women, no less than that of men, should be adapted to modern needs and should provide sufficient time and suitable institutional opportunities for a systematic education, extending to all areas, from the theological-pastoral to the professional. Pastoral and catechetical formation, always important, is particularly relevant in view of the new evangelization, which calls for new forms of participation also on the part of women.

Clearly, a more solid formation, while helping consecrated women to understand better their own gifts, cannot but encourage within the Church the reciprocity which is needed. In the field of theological, cultural, and spiritual studies, much can be expected from the genius of women, not only in relation to specific aspects of feminine consecrated life, but also in understanding the faith in all its expressions. In this regard, the history of spirituality owes much to saints like Teresa of Jesus and Catherine of Siena, the first two women to be given the title "Doctor of the Church," and to so many other mystics for their exploration of the mystery of God and their analysis of his action in believers! The Church depends a great deal on consecrated women for new efforts in fostering Christian doctrine and morals, family and social life, and especially in everything that affects the dignity of women and respect for human life.[131] In fact, "*women* occupy a place, in thought and action, which is unique and decisive. It depends on them to promote a 'new feminism' which rejects the temptation of imitating models of 'male domination,' in order to acknowledge and affirm the true genius of women in every aspect of the life of society, and overcome all discrimination, violence, and exploitation."[132]

There is reason to hope that a fuller acknowledgment of the mission of women will provide feminine consecrated life with a heightened awareness of its specific role and increased dedication to the cause of the Kingdom of God. This will be expressed in many different works, such as involvement in evangelization, educational activities, participation in the formation of future priests and consecrated persons, animating Christian communities, giving spiritual support, and promoting the fundamental values of life and peace. To consecrated women and their extraordinary capacity for dedication, I once again express the gratitude and admiration of the whole Church, which supports them so that they will live their vocation fully and joyfully, and feel called to the great task of helping to educate the woman of today.

Ponder

The Extraordinary Synod of Bishops held in 1985 stated that the "ecclesiology of communion is the central and fundamental idea in the documents of the council."* In this chapter of Vita Consecrata, John Paul II takes up that idea and considers its importance for the consecrated life. He begins with the strong theological foundation he set up in the first chapter, by emphasizing the role of the Trinity. The communion or bonds of love in the Church are a reflection of this mystery. In particular, the consecrated life forms "a human community in which the Trinity dwells, in order to extend in history the gifts of communion proper to the three divine Persons" (no. 41).

It's worthwhile to think about how each Person of the Trinity inspires communion of life. It comes about from the initiative of God the Father, who sent the Son into the world. By his life of love and dedication, Jesus not only gave us an example but actually communicates grace to us, so that we can follow him and live as he taught us. Jesus sent the Spirit to pour love into our hearts, which overflows onto others. A community of consecrated persons does not come into being from a utilitarian motive, but as John Paul II says, is "a God-enlightened space in which to experience the hidden presence of the Risen Lord" (no. 42). The love that unites the members of the community is fruitful and goes out to others in a

---

* The Final Report of the Extraordinary Synod of Bishops, 1985, II, C., 1.

mission prompted by the Spirit. It's somewhat analogous to the love of a man and a woman who marry and whose love brings forth children.

This love forms the basis of communion and reflects the ideal Christian community presented in the Acts of the Apostles: "They devoted themselves to the apostles' teaching and fellowship, to the breaking of bread and the prayers. . . . All who believed were together and had all things in common" (Acts 2:42, 4). The whole Church is a communion, sharing the gifts of grace that flow from Christ and the Holy Spirit. Throughout this long section, John Paul II speaks of different ways communion is developed in the consecrated life. Communities form bonds of communion not only among themselves but with other communities and with the Church's pastors. It also extends to the lay faithful, who can be invited to cooperate in the mission carried out by consecrated persons.

The Pope speaks in general terms in a document intended for the whole Church. Each community can apply it to their own situation. Yet John Paul II gives an important principle when he says, "*sharing in the Trinitarian communion can change human relationships* and create a new type of solidarity" (no. 41). As human beings we are the image of God not only because we have reason and free will, but also because as persons we can relate to other persons. This is an image of the communion among the Persons of the Trinity. Speaking of the creation account in Genesis, John Paul II said that the human person "becomes an image of God not so much in the moment of solitude as in the moment of communion" (TOB 9:3). This image grows even deeper through the grace of Jesus Christ, which enables us to participate in the very life of the Trinity. Each member of a community is the image of God, and when joined with the other members, the community itself shows forth the face of Christ to the world.

1. The Pope presents a high, even exalted, vision of what a community of consecrated persons ought to look like. Yet we all suffer from human weaknesses that can make communal living a struggle and even a cross. If you live in a community, how do you reconcile these two realities? How can you integrate the negative so that it does not become a source of bitterness and discouragement, but an opportunity to grow even more in love?

2. Today we live in an atmosphere affected by individualism, which can lead to a spirit of entitlement. How do you balance a legitimate concern for your own needs with the common good? If there is a conflict, are you willing to sacrifice some of your own interests for the sake of others?

3. John Paul II treats many topics in this long section, such as the role of authority, thinking with the Church, cooperation with the laity, the unique role of women, and others. Which of these topics is especially important to you? If you could dialogue with John Paul II about it, what would you wish to say or ask him?

Pray

The Acts of the Apostles presents the early Christian community as filled with the fervor and love inspired by the Holy Spirit. Yet even then problems arose. Spend some time reading and praying with Acts 15:1–41, which describes the controversy over circumcision for the Gentiles, and Paul's disagreement with Barnabas. What can we learn from this about resolving our present conflicts? Ask the Holy Spirit for the light you might need to deal with any troublesome issue in your life or that of your community or family.

Act

Do one thing today to lighten someone else's burden. It can be as simple as taking out the garbage, helping with kitchen cleanup, or doing some other hidden task.

II. Continuity in the Work of the Spirit: Faithfulness in the Course of Change

Cloistered nuns

59. The monastic life of women and the cloister deserve special attention because of the great esteem in which the Christian community holds this type of life, which is a sign of the exclusive union of the Church as Bride with her Lord, whom she loves above all things. Indeed, the life of cloistered nuns, devoted in a special way to prayer, to asceticism and diligent progress in the spiritual life, "is nothing other than a journey to the heavenly Jerusalem and an anticipation of the eschatological Church immutable in its possession and contemplation of God."[133] In the light of this vocation and ecclesial mission, the cloister responds to the need, felt as paramount, *to be with the Lord*. Choosing an enclosed space where they will live their lives, cloistered nuns share in Christ's emptying of himself by means of a radical poverty, expressed in their renunciation not only of this but also of "space," of contacts, of so many benefits of creation. This particular way of offering up the "body" allows them to enter more fully into the Eucharistic mystery. They offer themselves with Jesus for the world's salvation. Their offering, besides its elements of sacrifice and expiation, takes on the aspect of thanksgiving to the Father, by sharing in the thanksgiving of the beloved Son.

Rooted in this profound spiritual aspiration, the cloister is not only an ascetic practice of very great value but also *a way of living Christ's Passover*.[134] From being an experience of "death," it becomes a superabundance of life, representing a joyful proclamation and prophetic anticipation of the possibility offered to every person and to the whole of humanity to live solely for God in Christ Jesus (cf. Rom 6:11). The cloister brings to mind that *space in the heart* where every person is called to union with the Lord. Accepted as a gift and chosen as a free response of love, the cloister is the place of spiritual communion with God and with the brethren, where the limitation of space and contacts works to the advantage of interiorizing Gospel values (cf. Jn 13:34; Mt 5:3, 8).

Even in the simplicity of their life, cloistered communities, set like cities on a hilltop or lights on a lampstand (cf. Mt 5:14–15), visibly represent the goal toward which the entire community of the Church travels. "Eager to act and yet devoted to contemplation,"[135] the Church advances down the paths of time with her eyes fixed on the future restoration of all things in Christ, when she will appear "in glory with her Spouse" (cf. Col 3:1–4),[136] and Christ will deliver "the Kingdom to God the Father after destroying every rule and every authority and power . . . that God may be everything to everyone" (1 Cor 15:24, 28).

To these dear Sisters, therefore, I extend my gratitude and I encourage them to remain faithful to the cloistered life according to their particular charism. Thanks to their example, this way of life continues to draw many vocations, attracting people by the radical nature of a "spousal" existence dedicated totally to God in contemplation. As an expression of pure love which is worth more than any work, the contemplative life generates an extraordinary apostolic and missionary effectiveness.[137]

The Synod Fathers expressed great esteem for the cloistered life, while at the same time giving attention to requests made by some with respect to its concrete discipline. The Synod's suggestions in this regard and especially the desire that provision be made for giving major superiors more authority to grant dispensations from enclosure for just and grave reasons,[138] will be carefully considered, in the light of the path of renewal already undertaken since the Second Vatican Council.[139] In this way, the various forms and degrees of cloister—from papal and constitutional cloister to monastic cloister—will better correspond to the variety of contemplative institutes and monastic traditions.

As the Synod itself emphasized, *associations* and *federations* of monasteries are to be encouraged, as already recommended by Pope Pius XII and the Second Vatican Council,[140] especially where there are no other effective forms of coordination or help, with a view to safeguarding and promoting the values of contemplative life. Such bodies, which must always respect the legitimate autonomy of monasteries, can in fact offer valuable help in adequately resolving common problems, such as appropriate renewal, initial and continuing formation, mutual economic support, and even the reorganization of the monasteries themselves.

Religious brothers

60. According to the traditional doctrine of the Church, the consecrated life by its nature *is neither lay nor clerical*.[141] For this reason the "lay consecration" of both men and women constitutes a state which in its profession of the evangelical

counsels is complete in itself.[142] Consequently, both for the individual and for the Church, it is a value in itself, apart from the sacred ministry.

Following the teaching of the Second Vatican Council,[143] the Synod expressed great esteem for the kind of consecrated life in which religious brothers provide valuable services of various kinds, inside or outside the community, participating in this way in the mission of proclaiming the Gospel and bearing witness to it with charity in everyday life. Indeed, some of these services can be considered *ecclesial ministries*, granted by legitimate authority. This requires an appropriate and integral formation: human, spiritual, theological, pastoral, and professional.

According to the terminology currently in use, institutes which, by reason of their founders' design or by legitimate tradition, have a character and purpose which do not entail the exercise of Holy Orders are called "lay institutes."[144] Nonetheless the Synod pointed out that this terminology does not adequately express the particular nature of the vocation of the members of these religious institutes. In fact, although they perform many works in common with the lay faithful, these men do so insofar as they are consecrated, and thereby express the spirit of total self-giving to Christ and the Church, in accordance with their specific charism.

For this reason the Synod Fathers, in order to avoid ambiguity and confusion with the secular state of the lay faithful,[145] proposed the term *religious institutes of brothers*.[146] This proposal is significant, especially when we consider that the term "brother" suggests a rich spirituality. "These religious are called to be brothers of Christ, deeply united with him, 'the firstborn among many brothers' (Rom 8:29), brothers to one another, in mutual love and working together in the Church in the same service of what is good; brothers to everyone, in their witness to Christ's love for all, especially the lowliest, the neediest; brothers for a greater brotherhood in the Church."[147] By living in a special way this aspect of Christian and consecrated life, religious brothers are an effective reminder to religious priests themselves of the fundamental dimension of brotherhood in Christ, to be lived among themselves and with every man and woman, and they proclaim to all the Lord's words: "And you are all brothers" (Mt 23:8).

In these religious institutes of brothers nothing prevents certain members from receiving Holy Orders for the priestly service of the religious community, provided that this is approved by the General Chapter.[148] However, the Second Vatican Council does not give any explicit encouragement for this, precisely because it wishes institutes of brothers to remain faithful to their vocation and mission. The same holds true with regard to assuming the office of superior, since that office reflects in a special way the nature of the institute itself.

The vocation of brothers in what are known as "clerical" institutes is different, since, according to the design of the founder or by reason of legitimate tradition, these institutes presuppose the exercise of Holy Orders, are governed by clerics, and as such are approved by Church authority.[149] In these institutes the sacred ministry is constitutive of the charism itself and determines its nature, purpose and spirit. The presence of brothers constitutes a different form of participation in an institute's mission, through services rendered both within the community and in the apostolate, in collaboration with those who exercise the priestly ministry.

Mixed institutes

61. Some religious institutes, which in the founder's original design were envisaged as a brotherhood in which all the members, priests and those who were not priests, were considered equal among themselves, have acquired a different form with the passing of time. It is necessary that these institutes, known as "mixed," evaluate on the basis of a deeper understanding of their founding charism whether it is appropriate and possible to return to their original inspiration.

The Synod Fathers expressed the hope that in these institutes all the religious would be recognized as having equal rights and obligations, with the exception of those which stem from Holy Orders.[150] A special commission has been established to examine and resolve the problems connected with this issue; it is necessary to await this commission's conclusions before coming to suitable decisions in accordance with what will be authoritatively determined.

New forms of the evangelical life

62. The Spirit, who at different times has inspired numerous forms of consecrated life, does not cease to assist the Church, whether by fostering in already existing institutes a commitment to renewed faithfulness to the founding charism, or by giving new charisms to men and women of our own day so that they can start institutions responding to the challenges

of our times. A sign of this divine intervention is to be found in the so-called *new foundations*, which display new characteristics compared to those of traditional foundations.

The originality of the new communities often consists in the fact that they are composed of mixed groups of men and women, of clerics and lay persons, of married couples and celibates, all of whom pursue a particular style of life. These communities are sometimes inspired by one or other traditional form adapted to the needs of modern society. Their commitment to the evangelical life also takes on different forms, while, as a general rule, they are all characterized by an intense aspiration to community life, poverty, and prayer. Both clerics and lay persons share in the duties of governing according to the responsibilities assigned to them, and the apostolate focuses on the demands of the new evangelization.

If, on one hand, there is reason to rejoice at the Holy Spirit's action, there is, on the other, a need for *discernment regarding these charisms*. A fundamental principle, when speaking of the consecrated life, is that the specific features of the new communities and their styles of life must be founded on the essential theological and canonical elements proper to the consecrated life.[151] This discernment is necessary at both the local and universal level, in order to manifest a common obedience to the one Spirit. In dioceses, bishops should examine the witness of life and the orthodoxy of the founders of such communities, their spirituality, the ecclesial awareness shown in carrying out their mission, the methods of formation, and the manner of incorporation into the community. They should wisely evaluate possible weaknesses, watching patiently for the sign of results (cf. Mt 7:16), so that they may acknowledge the authenticity of the charism.[152] In a special way, bishops are required to determine, according to clearly established criteria, the suitability of any members of these communities who wish to receive Holy Orders.[153]

Worthy of praise are those forms of commitment which some Christian married couples assume in certain associations and movements. They confirm by means of a vow the obligation of chastity proper to the married state and, without neglecting their duties toward their children, profess poverty and obedience.[154] They do so with the intention of bringing to the perfection of charity their love, already "consecrated" in the sacrament of Matrimony.[155] However, by reason of the above-mentioned principle of discernment, these forms of commitment cannot be included in the specific category of the consecrated life. This necessary clarification regarding the nature of such experiences in no way intends to underestimate this particular path of holiness, from which the action of the Holy Spirit, infinitely rich in gifts and inspirations, is certainly not absent.

In view of such a wealth of gifts and creative energies, it seems appropriate *to set up a commission to deal with questions relating to new forms of consecrated life.* The purpose of this commission will be to determine criteria of authenticity which will help discernment and decision-making.[156] Among its other tasks, this commission will evaluate, in the light of the experience of recent decades, which new forms of consecration can, with pastoral prudence and to the advantage of all, be officially approved by Church authority, in order to be proposed to the faithful who are seeking a more perfect Christian life.

New associations of evangelical life *are not alternatives* to already existing institutions, which continue to hold the pre-eminent place assigned to them by tradition. Nonetheless, the new forms are also a gift of the Spirit, enabling the Church to follow her Lord in a constant outpouring of generosity, attentive to God's invitations revealed through the signs of the times. Thus the Church appears before the world with many forms of holiness and service, as "a kind of instrument or sign of intimate union with God, and of the unity of mankind."[157] The older institutes, many of which have been tested by the severest of hardships, which they have accepted courageously down the centuries, can be enriched through dialogue and an exchange of gifts with the foundations appearing in our own day.

In this way the vigor of the different forms of consecrated life, from the oldest to the most recent, as well as the vitality of the new communities, will renew faithfulness to the Holy Spirit, who is the source of communion and unceasing newness of life.

III. *Looking to the Future*

Difficulties and future prospects

63. The changes taking place in society and the decrease in the number of vocations are weighing heavily on the consecrated life in some regions of the world. The apostolic works of many institutes and their very presence in certain local Churches are endangered. As has already occurred at other

times in history, there are institutes which even run the risk of disappearing altogether. The universal Church is profoundly grateful for the great contribution which these institutes have made to building her up through their witness and service.[158] The trials of the present do not take away from their merits and the positive results of their efforts.

For other institutes, there is the problem of reassessing their apostolate. This task, which is difficult and often painful, requires study and discernment in the light of certain criteria. For example, it is necessary to safeguard the significance of an institute's own charism, to foster community life, to be attentive to the needs of both the universal and particular Church, to show concern for what the world neglects, and to respond generously and boldly to the new forms of poverty through concrete efforts, even if necessarily on a small scale, and above all in the most abandoned areas.[159]

The various difficulties stemming from the decline in personnel and apostolates *must in no way lead to a loss of confidence in the evangelical vitality of the consecrated life*, which will always be present and active in the Church. While individual institutes have no claim to permanence, the consecrated life itself will continue to sustain among the faithful the response of love toward God and neighbor. Thus it is necessary to distinguish the *historical destiny* of a specific institute or form of consecrated life from the *ecclesial mission* of the consecrated life as such. The former is affected by changing circumstances; the latter is destined to perdure.

This is true of both the contemplative and apostolic forms of consecrated life. On the whole, under the ever-creative guidance of the Spirit, the consecrated life is destined to remain a shining witness to the inseparable unity of love of God and love of neighbor. It appears as the living memory of the fruitfulness of God's love. New situations of difficulty are therefore to be faced with the serenity of those who know that what is required of each individual is *not success, but commitment to faithfulness*. What must be avoided at all costs is the actual breakdown of the consecrated life, a collapse which is not measured by a decrease in numbers but by a failure to cling steadfastly to the Lord and to personal vocation and mission. Rather, by persevering faithfully in the consecrated life, consecrated persons confess with great effectiveness before the world their unwavering trust in the Lord of history, in whose hands are the history and destiny of individuals, institutions, and peoples, and therefore also the realization in time of his gifts. Sad situations of crisis invite consecrated persons courageously to proclaim their faith in Christ's death and resurrection, that they may become a visible sign of the passage from death to life.

Fresh efforts in the promotion of vocations

64. The mission of the consecrated life, as well as the vitality of institutes, undoubtedly depend on the faithful commitment with which consecrated persons respond to their vocation. But they have a future to the extent that *still other men and women generously welcome the Lord's call*. The problem of vocations is a real challenge which directly concerns the various institutes but also involves the whole Church. Great spiritual and material energies are being expended in the

sphere of vocational promotion, but the results do not always match expectations and efforts. Thus, while vocations to the consecrated life are flourishing in the young Churches and in those which suffered persecution at the hands of totalitarian regimes, they are lacking in countries traditionally rich in vocations, including vocations for the missions.

This difficult situation puts consecrated persons to the test. Sometimes they ask themselves: Have we perhaps lost the capacity to attract new vocations? They must have confidence in the Lord Jesus, who continues to call men and women to follow him. They must entrust themselves to the Holy Spirit, who inspires and bestows the charisms of the consecrated life. Therefore, while we rejoice in the action of the Spirit, who rejuvenates the Bride of Christ by enabling the consecrated life to flourish in many nations, we must also pray unceasingly to the Lord of the harvest, that he will send workers to his Church in order to meet the needs of the new evangelization (cf. Mt 9:37–38). Besides promoting prayer for vocations, it is essential to act, by means of explicit presentation and appropriate catechesis, with a view to encouraging in those called to the consecrated life that free, willing, and generous response which carries into effect the grace of vocation.

The invitation of Jesus, "Come and see" (Jn 1:39), is *the golden rule* of pastoral work for promoting vocations, even today. Following the example of founders and foundresses, this work aims at presenting *the attraction of the person of the Lord Jesus* and the beauty of the total gift of self for the sake of the Gospel. A primary responsibility of all consecrated men and women is therefore to propose with courage, by word and example, the ideal of the following of Christ, and then to support the response to the Spirit's action in the heart of those who are called.

After the enthusiasm of the first meeting with Christ, there comes the constant struggle of everyday life, a struggle which turns a vocation into a tale of friendship with the Lord. In view of this, the pastoral work of promoting vocations should make use of suitable help, such as *spiritual direction*, in order to nourish that personal response of love of the Lord which is the necessary condition for becoming disciples and apostles of his Kingdom. Moreover, if the flourishing of vocations evident in some parts of the world justifies optimism and hope, the lack of them in other areas must not lead either to discouragement or to the temptation to practice lax and unwise recruitment. The task of promoting vocations should increasingly express *a joint commitment of the whole Church*.[160] It calls for the active collaboration of pastors, religious, families, and teachers, as required in something which forms an integral part of the overall pastoral plan of every particular Church. In every diocese there should be this *common endeavor*, which coordinates and promotes the efforts of everyone, not jeopardizing, but rather supporting, the vocational activity of each institute.[161]

The effective cooperation of the whole People of God, with the support of Providence, cannot but give rise to an abundance of divine gifts. Christian solidarity should abound in meeting the needs of vocational formation in countries which are economically poorer. The recruitment of vocations in these countries should be carried out by the various institutes in full accord with the Churches of the region, and on the basis of an active and long-term involvement in their pastoral life.[162] The most authentic way to support the Spirit's action is for institutes to invest their best resources generously in vocational work, especially by their serious involvement in working with youth.

Commitment to initial formation

65. The Synod Assembly paid special attention to the formation of those who wish to consecrate themselves to the Lord,[163] and recognized its decisive importance. The *primary objective* of the formation process is to prepare people for the total consecration of themselves to God in the following of Christ, at the service of the Church's mission. To say "yes" to the Lord's call by taking personal responsibility for maturing in one's vocation is the inescapable duty of all who have been called. One's whole life must be open to the action of the Holy Spirit, traveling the road of formation with generosity, and accepting in faith the means of grace offered by the Lord and the Church.[164]

Formation should therefore have a profound effect on individuals, so that their every attitude and action, at important moments as well as in the ordinary events of life, will show that they belong completely and joyfully to God.[165] Since the very purpose of consecrated life is conformity to the Lord Jesus in his *total self-giving*,[166] this must also be the principal objective of formation. Formation is a path of gradual identification with the attitude of Christ toward the Father.

If this is the purpose of the consecrated life, the manner of preparing for it should include and express *the character of wholeness*. Formation should involve the whole person,[167] in every aspect of the personality, in behavior and intentions. Precisely because it aims at the transformation of the whole person, it is clear that *the commitment to formation never ends*. Indeed, at every stage of life, consecrated persons must be offered opportunities to grow in their commitment to the charism and mission of their institute.

For formation to be complete, it must include every aspect of Christian life. It must therefore provide a human, cultural, spiritual, and pastoral preparation which pays special attention to the harmonious integration of all its various aspects. Sufficient time should be reserved for initial formation, understood as a process of development which passes through every stage of personal maturity—from the psychological and spiritual to the theological and pastoral. In the case of those studying for the priesthood, this initial formation coincides with and fits well into a specific course of studies, as part of a broader formation program.

The work of those responsible for formation

66. God the Father, through the unceasing gift of Christ and the Spirit, is the educator *par excellence* of those who consecrate themselves to him. But in this work he makes use of human instruments, placing more mature brothers and sisters at the side of those whom he calls. Formation then is a sharing in the work of the Father who, through the Spirit, fashions the inner attitudes of the Son in the hearts of young men and

women. Those in charge of formation must therefore be very familiar with the path of seeking God, so as to be able to accompany others on this journey.

Sensitive to the action of grace, they will also be able to point out those obstacles which are less obvious. But above all they will disclose the beauty of following Christ and the value of the charism by which this is accomplished. They will combine the illumination of spiritual wisdom with the light shed by human means, which can be a help both in discerning the call and in forming the new man or woman, until they are genuinely free. The chief instrument of formation is personal dialogue, a practice of irreplaceable and commendable effectiveness which should take place regularly and with a certain frequency.

Because sensitive tasks are involved, the training of suitable directors of formation, who will fulfill their task in a spirit of communion with the whole Church, is very important. It will be helpful to establish appropriate structures for *the training of those responsible for formation*, preferably in places where they can be in contact with the culture in which their pastoral service will later be carried out. In the work of formation, the more solidly established institutes should help those of more recent foundation by contributing some of their best members.[168]

Formation in community and for the apostolate

67. Since formation must also have a *communal* dimension, the community is the chief place of formation in institutes of consecrated life and societies of apostolic life. Initiation

into the hardships and joys of community life takes place in the community itself. Through the fraternal life each one learns to live with those whom God has put at his or her side, accepting their positive traits along with their differences and limitations. Each one learns to share the gifts received for the building up of all, because "to each is given the manifestation of the Spirit for the common good" (1 Cor 12:7).[169] At the same time, from the moment of initial formation, community life must disclose the essential missionary dimension of consecration. Thus, during the period of initial formation, institutes of consecrated life do well to provide practical experiences which are prudently followed by the one responsible for formation, enabling candidates to test, in the context of the local culture, their skills for the apostolate, their ability to adapt, and their spirit of initiative.

On the one hand, it is important for consecrated persons gradually to develop a critical judgment, based on the Gospel, regarding the positive and negative values of their own culture and of the culture in which they will eventually work. On the other hand, they must be trained in the difficult art of interior harmony, of the interaction between love of God and love of one's brothers and sisters; they must likewise learn that prayer is the soul of the apostolate, but also that the apostolate animates and inspires prayer.

The need for a complete and updated "ratio"

68. A definite period of formation extending up to final profession is recommended both for women's institutes, and

for men's institutes as regards religious brothers. Essentially, this is also true for cloistered communities, which ought to set up suitable programs, aimed at imparting a genuine preparation for the contemplative life and its particular mission in the Church.

The Synod Fathers earnestly asked all institutes of consecrated life and societies of apostolic life to draw up as soon as possible a *ratio institutionis*, that is, a formation program inspired by their particular charism, presenting clearly and in all its stages the course to be followed in order to assimilate fully the spirituality of the respective institute. The *ratio* responds to a pressing need today. On the one hand, it shows how to pass on the institute's spirit so that it will be lived in its integrity by future generations, in different cultures and geographical regions; on the other hand, it explains to consecrated persons how to live that spirit in the different stages of life on the way to full maturity of faith in Christ.

While it is true that the renewal of the consecrated life depends primarily on formation, it is equally certain that this training is, in turn, linked to the ability to establish a method characterized by spiritual and pedagogical wisdom, which will gradually lead those wishing to consecrate themselves to put on the mind of Christ the Lord. Formation is a dynamic process by means of which individuals are converted to the Word of God in the depths of their being and, at the same time, learn how to discover the signs of God in earthly realities. At a time when religious values are increasingly being ignored by society, this plan of formation is doubly important: as a result of it, consecrated persons will not only continue to "see" God with the eyes of faith in a world which ignores his presence, but will also be effective in making his presence in some way "perceptible" through the witness of their charism.

Continuing formation

69. Continuing formation, whether in institutes of apostolic or contemplative life, is an intrinsic requirement of religious consecration. As mentioned above, the formation process is not limited to the initial phase. Due to human limitations, the consecrated person can never claim to have completely brought to life the "new creature" who, in every circumstance of life, reflects the very mind of Christ. *Initial* formation, then, should be closely connected with *continuing* formation, thereby creating a readiness on everyone's part to let themselves be formed every day of their lives.[170]

Consequently, it will be very important for every institute to provide, as part of its *ratio institutionis*, a precise and systematic description of its plan of continuing formation. The chief purpose of this plan is to provide all consecrated persons with a program which encompasses their whole life. None are exempt from the obligation to grow humanly and as religious; by the same token, no one can be over-confident and live in self-sufficient isolation. At no stage of life can people feel so secure and committed that they do not need to give careful attention to ensuring perseverance in faithfulness; just as there is no age at which a person has completely achieved maturity.

In a constant search for faithfulness

70. There is a youthfulness of spirit which lasts through time; it arises from the fact that at every stage of life a person seeks and finds a new task to fulfill, a particular way of being, of serving, and of loving.[171]

In the consecrated life *the first years of full involvement in the apostolate* are a critical stage, marked by the passage from a supervised life to a situation of *full responsibility for one's work*. It is important that young consecrated persons be supported and accompanied by a brother or sister who helps them to live to the full the freshness of their love and enthusiasm for Christ.

The next stage can present *the risk of routine*, and the subsequent temptation to give in to disappointment because of meager results. Middle-aged consecrated persons must therefore be helped, in the light of the Gospel and the charism of their institute, to renew their original decision, and not confuse the completeness of their dedication with the degree of good results. This will enable them to give a fresh impulse and new motivations to their decision. This is the time to search for what is essential.

The stage of maturity, while it brings personal growth, can also bring *the danger of a certain individualism*, accompanied either by a fear of not being in line with the times, or by forms of inflexibility, self-centeredness, or diminished enthusiasm. At this point continuing formation is aimed at helping not only to bring back a higher level of spiritual and apostolic life, but also at discovering the special characteristics of this stage of life. For at this time, after refining certain features of the personality, the gift of self is made to God more genuinely and with greater generosity; it extends to others with greater serenity and wisdom, as well as with greater simplicity and richness of grace. This is the gift and experience of spiritual fatherhood and motherhood.

Advanced age poses new problems, which can be prepared for by a discerning program of spiritual support. The gradual withdrawal from activity, sometimes caused by sickness or forced immobility, can be a very formative experience. Often a time of suffering, advanced age nonetheless offers to elderly consecrated persons the chance to be transformed by the Paschal experience[172] by being configured to the crucified Christ, who fulfills the Father's will in all things and abandons himself into the Father's hands, even to the surrendering of his spirit to him. This configuration represents a new way of living one's consecration, which is not tied to effectiveness in carrying out administrative responsibilities or apostolic work.

When *the moment finally comes for uniting oneself to the supreme hour of the Lord's Passion*, the consecrated person knows that the Father is now bringing to completion the mysterious process of formation which began many years before. Death will then be awaited and prepared for as the supreme act of love and self-offering.

It should be added that, independently of the different stages of life, any period can present critical situations due to external factors—such as a change of place or assignment, difficulties in work or lack of success in the apostolate, misunderstandings and feelings of alienation—or resulting from more directly personal factors such as physical or mental illness, spiritual aridity, deaths, difficulties in interpersonal relations, strong temptations, crises of faith or identity, or feelings of uselessness. When fidelity becomes more difficult, the individual must be offered the support of greater trust and deeper love, at both the personal and community levels. At such times, the sensitive closeness of the superior is most essential. Great comfort can also come from the valuable help of a brother or sister, whose concerned and caring presence can lead to a rediscovery of the meaning of the covenant which God originally established, and which he has no intention of breaking. The person undergoing such a trial will then accept purification and hardship as essential to the following of Christ crucified. The trial itself will appear as a providential means of being formed by the Father's hands, and as a struggle which is not only *psychological*, carried out by the "I" in relation to itself and its weaknesses, but also *religious*, touched each day by the presence of God and the power of the cross!

Dimensions of continuing formation

71. If the subject of formation is the individual at every stage of life, the object of formation is the whole person, called to seek and love God "with all one's heart, and with all one's soul, and with all one's might" (cf. Dt 6:5), and one's neighbor as oneself (cf. Lev 19:18; Mt 22:37–39). Love of God and of the brethren is a powerful force which can ceaselessly inspire the process of growth and fidelity. *Life in the Spirit* is clearly of primary importance. Living in the Spirit, consecrated persons discover their own identity and find profound peace; they grow more attentive to the daily challenges of the word of

God, and they allow themselves to be guided by the original inspiration of their institute. Under the action of the Spirit, they resolutely keep times for prayer, silence, and solitude, and they never cease to ask the Almighty for the gift of wisdom in the struggles of everyday life (cf. Wis 9:10).

The human and fraternal dimensions of the consecrated life call for self-knowledge and the awareness of personal limitations, so as to offer its members the inspiration and support needed on the path toward perfect freedom. In present day circumstances, special importance must be given to the interior freedom of consecrated persons, their affective maturity, their ability to communicate with others, especially in their own community, their serenity of spirit, their compassion for those who are suffering, their love for the truth, and a correspondence between their actions and their words.

The apostolic dimension opens the hearts and minds of consecrated persons and prepares them for constant effort in the apostolate, as the sign that it is the love of Christ which urges them on (cf. 2 Cor 5:14). In practice, this will involve updating the methods and objectives of apostolic works in fidelity to the spirit and aims of the founder or foundress and to subsequently emerging traditions, with continuous attention to changing historical and cultural conditions, at the general and local levels where the apostolate is carried out.

The cultural and professional dimensions, based upon a solid theological training which provides the means for wise discernment, involve continual updating and special interest in the different areas to which each charism is directed. Consecrated persons must therefore keep themselves as intellectually open and adaptable as possible, so that the apostolate will be envisaged and carried out according to the needs of their own time, making use of the means provided by cultural progress.

Finally, all these elements are united *in the dimension of the charism* proper to each institute, as it were in a synthesis which calls for a constant deepening of one's own special consecration in all its aspects, not only apostolic but also ascetical and mystical. This means that each member should study diligently the spirit, history, and mission of the institute to which he or she belongs, in order to advance the personal and communal assimilation of its charism.[173]

Ponder

In these two sections John Paul II considers some particular types of consecrated life and their prospects for the future. First he mentions cloistered nuns, speaking of the value of this type of contemplative life, which is not always understood by a world that highlights activity. But both the Church and the world need this powerhouse of prayer, of persons who dedicate themselves to interceding for others. In this context the Pope speaks of "the radical nature of a 'spousal' existence dedicated totally to God in contemplation" (no. 59).

Spousal existence is a familiar theme in John Paul II's theology of the body. He says that every human person is called to make a gift of self, which is a spousal gift. But the gift can be realized in different ways. Those called to marriage make an exclusive self-gift to one's spouse. Those called to the consecrated life make an exclusive self-gift directly to God. It then flows out to others in mission. The Pope stresses over and over that we find our happiness and fulfillment not by a selfish striving for our own interests, but by making a gift of ourselves to others in love.

In number 60 the Pope speaks about religious brothers. Despite their small numbers they are an important part of the consecrated life, a group that is often overlooked. They make an invaluable contribution to many of the Church's ministries. The Pope also clarifies some terminology based on input from the Synod. While sometimes called "lay institutes," a better term to refer to congregations of brothers is "religious institutes of brothers." They were called "lay" in the sense that they were not ordained, but this can obscure the true nature of their vocation as an important part of the consecrated life. As mentioned earlier, the consecrated life is a unique vocation, distinct from that of the laity and of the ordained.

The Pope then speaks of new forms of the consecrated life that are appearing in our time. While we can rejoice at the way the Holy Spirit is working in the Church, we also need to carefully discern these new charisms. Some will flourish, but others may not. In this time of ferment, while some new groups are appearing, others are struggling. In Chapter III, John Paul II speaks frankly of the difficulties facing many institutes. He says, "What must be avoided at all costs is the actual breakdown of the consecrated life, a collapse which is not measured by a decrease in numbers but by a failure to cling steadfastly to the Lord and to personal vocation and mission" (no. 63). Despite such problems we still have reasons for hope, since the consecrated life "will always be present and active in the Church." No doubt future historians will look back to our era and see it not only as a time of upheaval in the consecrated life, but one that is also full of hope and promise. While we are living through it, we can't see how things will ultimately develop. But we do know that the Holy Spirit is continuing to breathe life into the Church and will bring about something that will endure for the Kingdom of God.

Finally, the Pope speaks of the need for initial and ongoing formation. As he says so beautifully, "After the enthusiasm of the first meeting with Christ, there comes the constant struggle of everyday life, a struggle which turns a vocation into a tale of friendship with the Lord" (no. 64). Each person called to the consecrated life needs to continue to grow in his or her vocation throughout one's entire life. Formation never ends.

1. In terms of the wide picture of consecrated life today, we see both lights and shadows, areas of struggle and areas of new growth. How do you think this relates to the Paschal Mystery and the way it is lived out in the Church in every age?

2. The Lord never ceases to call people to the consecrated life. What ideas do you have about how the Church can promote "the beauty of the total gift of self for the sake of the Gospel" (no. 63)?

3. In number 70, the Pope reviews the various stages of life and the gifts and challenges they present. How does this relate to where you are in your own life journey?

Pray

John Paul II says, "After the enthusiasm of the first meeting with Christ, there comes the constant struggle of everyday life" (no. 64). The Letter to the Hebrews has some beautiful passages of encouragement for Christians who were in danger of backsliding in their faith. Pray with Hebrews 10:32–39, recalling your own struggles and asking for the help you need to continue along the way.

ACT

The topic of formation, both initial and ongoing, takes up a good part of this section of the chapter. As the Pope notes, "there is no age at which a person has completely achieved maturity" (no. 69). What is one thing that you could do to grow in your own personal emotional and spiritual maturity?

CHAPTER III

Servitium Caritatis

Consecrated Life: Manifestation of God's Love in the World

Consecrated for mission

72. In the image of Jesus, the beloved Son "whom the Father consecrated and sent into the world" (Jn 10:36), those whom God calls to follow him are also consecrated and sent into the world to imitate his example and to continue his mission. Fundamentally, this is true of every disciple. In a special way, however, it is true of those who, in the manner that characterizes the consecrated life, are called to follow Christ "more closely," and to make him the "all" of their lives. The task of *devoting themselves wholly to "mission"* is therefore included in their call; indeed, by the action of the Holy Spirit who is at the origin of every vocation and charism, consecrated life itself is a mission, as was the whole of Jesus' life. The profession of the evangelical counsels, which makes a person totally free for the service of the Gospel, is important also from this point of view. It can therefore be said that *a sense of mission is essential*

to every institute, not only those dedicated to the active apostolic life, but also those dedicated to the contemplative life.

Indeed, more than in external works, the mission consists in making Christ present to the world through personal witness. This is the challenge, this is the primary task of the consecrated life! The more consecrated persons allow themselves to be conformed to Christ, the more Christ is made present and active in the world for the salvation of all.

Thus it can be said that consecrated persons are "in mission" by virtue of their very consecration, to which they bear witness in accordance with the ideal of their institute. When the founding charism provides for pastoral activities, it is obvious that the witness of life and the witness of works of the apostolate and human development are equally necessary: both mirror Christ who is at one and the same time consecrated to the glory of the Father and sent into the world for the salvation of his brothers and sisters.[174]

Religious life, moreover, continues the mission of Christ with another feature specifically its own: *fraternal life in community for the sake of the mission*. Thus, men and women religious will be all the more committed to the apostolate the more personal their dedication to the Lord Jesus is, the more fraternal their community life, and the more ardent their involvement in the institute's specific mission.

At the service of God and humanity

73. The consecrated life has the prophetic task *of recalling and serving the divine plan for humanity*, as it is announced in Scripture and as it emerges from an attentive reading of the

signs of God's providential action in history. This is the plan for the salvation and reconciliation of humanity (cf. Col 1:20–22). To carry out this service appropriately, consecrated persons must have a profound experience of God and be aware of the challenges of their time, understanding the profound theological meaning of these challenges through a discernment made with the help of the Spirit. In fact, it is often through historical events that we discern God's hidden call to work according to his plan by active and effective involvement in the events of our time.[175]

Discerning the signs of the times, as the Council affirms, must be done in the light of the Gospel, so as to "respond to the perennial questions which people ask about this present life and the life to come, and about the relationship of the one to the other."[176] It is necessary, therefore, to be open to the interior promptings of the Holy Spirit, who invites us to understand in depth the designs of Providence. He calls consecrated men and women to present new answers to the new problems of today's world. These are divine pleas which only souls accustomed to following God's will in everything can assimilate faithfully and then translate courageously into choices which are consistent with the original charism and which correspond to the demands of the concrete historical situation.

Faced with the many and pressing problems which sometimes seem to compromise or even overwhelm the consecrated life, those called to it cannot fail to feel the commitment to bear in their hearts and in their prayer the entire world's needs, while at the same time they work with zeal in the fields determined by the founding charism. Clearly, their dedication must be guided by *supernatural discernment*, which distinguishes what is of the Spirit from that which is contrary to him (cf. Gal 5:16–17, 22; 1 Jn 4:6). By means of fidelity to the rules and constitutions, this discernment safeguards full communion with the Church.[177]

In this way the consecrated life will not be limited to reading the signs of the times but will also contribute to elaborating and putting into effect *new initiatives of evangelization* for present-day situations. All this will be done in the certainty of faith that the Spirit can give satisfactory replies even to the most difficult questions. In this regard, we would do well to remember what the great champions of apostolic activity have always taught, namely, that we need to trust in God as if everything depended on him and, at the same time, to work generously as if everything depended on us.

Ecclesial cooperation and apostolic spirituality

74. Everything must be done *in communion and dialogue* with all other sectors of the Church. The challenges of evangelization are such that they cannot be effectively faced without the cooperation, both in discernment and action, of all the Church's members. It is difficult for individuals to provide a definitive answer, but such an answer can arise from encounter and dialogue. In particular, effective communion among those graced with different charisms will ensure both mutual enrichment and more fruitful results in the mission in hand. The experience of recent years widely confirms that "dialogue is the new name of charity,"[178] especially charity within the Church. Dialogue helps us to see the true implications of problems and

allows them to be addressed with greater hope of success. The consecrated life, by the very fact that it promotes the value of fraternal life, provides a privileged experience of dialogue. It can therefore contribute to creating a climate of mutual acceptance in which the Church's various components, feeling that they are valued for what they are, come together in ecclesial communion in a more convinced manner, ready to undertake the great universal mission.

Institutes involved in one or other form of the apostolate must therefore foster *a solid spirituality of action*, seeing God in all things and all things in God. In fact, "it is necessary to know that, just as a well-ordered life tends to pass from the active to the contemplative, so the soul generally returns with profit from the contemplative life to the active life, in order more perfectly to sustain the active life with the flame ignited in contemplation. Thus, the active life ought to lead to contemplation and, sometimes, from what we see interiorly, contemplation should more effectively call us back to action."[179] Jesus himself gave us the perfect example of how we can link communion with the Father to an intensely active life. Without a constant search for this unity, the danger of an interior breakdown, of confusion and discouragement, lurks always near. Today as yesterday, the close union between contemplation and action will allow the most difficult missions to be undertaken.

I. Love to the End

75. "Having loved his own who were in the world, he loved them to the end. And during supper . . . Jesus rose . . .

and began to wash the disciples' feet, and to wipe them with the towel with which he was girded" (Jn 13:1–2, 4–5).

In the washing of feet Jesus reveals the depth of God's love for humanity: in Jesus, God places himself at the service of human beings! At the same time, he reveals the meaning of the Christian life and, even more, of the consecrated life, which is *a life of self-giving love*, of practical and generous service. In its commitment to following the Son of Man, who "came not to be served but to serve" (Mt 20:28), the consecrated life, at least in the best periods of its long history, has been characterized by this "washing of feet," that is, by service directed in particular to the poorest and neediest. If, on the one hand, the consecrated life contemplates the sublime mystery of the Word in the bosom of the Father (cf. Jn 1:1), on the other hand it follows the Word who became flesh (cf. Jn 1:14), lowering himself, humbling himself in order to serve others. Even today, those who follow Christ on the path of the evangelical counsels intend to go where Christ went and to do what he did.

He continually calls new disciples to himself, both men and women, to communicate to them, by an outpouring of the Spirit (cf. Rom 5:5), the divine *agape*, his way of loving, and to urge them thus to serve others in the humble gift of themselves, far from all self-interest. Peter, overcome by the light of the transfiguration, exclaims: "Lord, it is well that we are here" (Mt 17:4), but he is invited to return to the byways of the world in order to continue serving the Kingdom of God: "Come down, Peter! You wanted to rest up on the mountain: come down. Preach the word of God, be insistent both when it is timely and when it is not; reprove, exhort, give encouragement using all your forbearance and ability to teach. Work, spend yourself, accept even sufferings and torments, in order that, through the brightness and beauty of good works, you may possess in charity what is symbolized in the Lord's white garments."[180] The fact that consecrated persons fix their gaze on the Lord's countenance does not diminish their commitment on behalf of humanity; on the contrary, it strengthens this commitment, enabling it to have an impact on history, in order to free history from all that disfigures it.

The quest for divine beauty impels consecrated persons to care for the deformed image of God on the faces of their brothers and sisters, faces disfigured by hunger, faces disillusioned by political promises, faces humiliated by seeing their culture despised, faces frightened by constant and indiscriminate violence, the anguished faces of minors, the hurt and humiliated faces of women, the tired faces of migrants who are not given a warm welcome, the faces of the elderly who are without even the minimum conditions for a dignified life.[181] The consecrated life thus shows, with the eloquence of works, that divine charity is the foundation and stimulus of freely given and active love. Saint Vincent de Paul was deeply convinced of this when he explained to the Daughters of Charity this program of life: "The spirit of the Society consists in giving yourselves to God in order to love our Lord and to serve him in the person of the materially and spiritually poor, in their houses and elsewhere, in order to teach poor young girls, children, in general anybody whom Divine Providence sends you."[182]

Today, among the possible works of charity, certainly the one which in a special way shows the world this love "to the end" is the fervent proclamation of Jesus Christ to those who do not yet know him, to those who have forgotten him, and to the poor in a preferential way.

The specific contribution of the consecrated life to evangelization

76. The specific contribution of consecrated persons, both men and women, to evangelization is first of all the witness of a life given totally to God and to their brothers and sisters in imitation of the Savior who, out of love for humanity, made himself a servant. In the work of salvation, in fact, everything comes from sharing in the divine *agape*. Consecrated persons make visible, in their consecration and total dedication, the loving and saving presence of Christ, the one consecrated by the Father, sent in mission.[183] Allowing themselves to be won over by him (cf. Phil 3:12), they prepare to become, in a certain way, a prolongation of his humanity.[184] The consecrated life eloquently shows that the more one lives in Christ, the better one can serve him in others, going even to the furthest missionary outposts and facing the greatest dangers.[185]

The first evangelization: proclaiming Christ to the nations

77. Those who love God, the Father of all, cannot fail to love their fellow human beings, whom they recognize as brothers and sisters. Precisely for this reason, they cannot

remain indifferent to the fact that many men and women do not know the full manifestation of God's love in Christ. The result, in obedience to Christ's commandment, is the missionary drive *ad gentes*, which every committed Christian shares with the Church which is missionary by nature. This drive is felt above all by the members of institutes, whether of the contemplative or of the active life.[186] Consecrated persons, in fact, have the task of making present even among non-Christians[187] Christ who is chaste, poor, obedient, prayerful, and missionary.[188] While remaining ever faithful to their charism they must know that they have a special share in the Church's missionary activity, in virtue of their interior consecration made to God.[189] The desire so often expressed by Thérèse of Lisieux, "to love you and make you loved," the ardent longing of Saint Francis Xavier that many, "meditating on what the Lord God will expect from them and from the talents he has given them, would be converted, using the right means and the spiritual exercises to know and feel within themselves the divine will, and so, adapting themselves more to that will than to their own inclinations, they would say: 'Lord, here I am, what do you want me to do? Lead me wherever you will,'"[190] and other similar testimonies of countless holy men and women, manifest the unsuppressible missionary drive which distinguishes and ennobles the consecrated life.

Present in every part of the world

78. "The love of Christ impels us" (2 Cor 5:14): the members of every institute should be able to repeat this truth with Saint Paul, because the task of the consecrated life is to work

in every part of the world in order to consolidate and expand the Kingdom of Christ, bringing the proclamation of the Gospel even to the most far off regions.[191] In fact, the history of the missions testifies to the great contribution made by consecrated men and women to the evangelization of peoples: from ancient monastic families to recent foundations committed exclusively to the mission *ad gentes*, from institutes of active life to those devoted to contemplation.[192] Countless consecrated persons have given their whole lives in this primary activity of the Church, which is "essential and never-ending"[193] because it is addressed to the growing number of those who do not know Christ.

Today too this duty continues to present a pressing call to institutes of consecrated life and societies of apostolic life: they are expected to make the greatest possible contribution to the proclamation of the Gospel of Christ. Also those institutes which are being established and are at work in the younger Churches are invited to open themselves to the mission among non-Christians, inside and outside their own countries of origin. Despite the understandable difficulties which some of them will meet, it is good to remind everyone that just as "faith is strengthened when it is given to others,"[194] so the mission strengthens the consecrated life, gives it new enthusiasm and new motivation, and elicits faithfulness. For its part, missionary activity offers ample room for all the different forms of the consecrated life.

The Church's mission *ad gentes* offers consecrated women, religious brothers, and members of secular institutes special and extraordinary opportunities for a particularly fruitful apostolate. The members of secular institutes, by their presence in fields more suited to the lay vocation, can engage in the valuable work of evangelizing all sectors of society, as well as the structures and the very laws which regulate it. Moreover, they can bear witness to Gospel values, living in contact with those who do not yet know Jesus, thus making a specific contribution to the mission.

It should be emphasized that in countries where non-Christian religions are firmly established, the presence of the consecrated life is of great importance, whether through its educational, charitable and cultural activities, or through the witness of the contemplative life. For this reason the establishment of communities devoted to contemplation should be encouraged in the new Churches, since "the contemplative life belongs to the fullness of the Church's presence."[195] It is necessary, then, to use appropriate means to foster an equitable distribution of the various forms of the consecrated life in order to give new momentum to evangelization, either by sending missionaries, or by institutes of consecrated life giving special help to poorer dioceses.[196]

The proclamation of Christ and inculturation

79. The proclamation of Christ "is the permanent priority of mission"[197] and is directed toward conversion, that is, to full and sincere allegiance to Christ and his Gospel.[198] In the context of missionary activity the process of inculturation and interreligious dialogue have a role to play. The challenge of inculturation ought to be taken up by consecrated persons as a call to fruitful cooperation with grace in facing cultural

diversity. This presupposes serious personal preparation, mature gifts of discernment, faithful adherence to the indispensable criteria of doctrinal orthodoxy, moral integrity and ecclesial communion.[199] Supported by the charism of their founders and foundresses, many consecrated persons have been able to approach cultures other than their own with the attitude of Jesus, who "emptied himself, taking the form of a servant" (Phil 2:7). With patient and courageous efforts to initiate dialogue, they have been successful in establishing contact with the most diverse peoples, proclaiming to all of them the way of salvation. Today too, many consecrated persons are looking for and are finding in the history of individuals and of entire peoples the traces of God's presence, a presence guiding all humanity toward the discernment of the signs of his saving will. Such a search proves to be advantageous for consecrated persons themselves: the values discovered in the different civilizations can in fact prompt them to deepen their own understanding of the Christian tradition of contemplation, community sharing, hospitality, respect for persons, and attention to the environment.

A genuine inculturation requires attitudes similar to those of the Lord when he became man and walked among us in love and meekness. In this sense the consecrated life makes its members particularly well suited to face the complex work of inculturation, because it accustoms them to being detached from things, even from many features of their own culture. Applying themselves with these attitudes to the study and understanding of other cultures, consecrated persons can better discern the real values in them, and the best way to accept them and perfect them with the help of their own charism.[200] However, it should not be forgotten that in many ancient cultures religious expression is so deeply ingrained that religion often represents the transcendent dimension of the culture itself. In this case true inculturation necessarily entails a serious and open interreligious dialogue, which "is not in opposition to the mission *ad gentes*" and "does not dispense from evangelization."[201]

The inculturation of the consecrated life

80. For its part, the consecrated life itself is the bearer of Gospel values and, where it is authentically lived, it can make an innovative contribution in meeting the challenges of inculturation. As a sign of the primacy of God and his Kingdom, it can, through dialogue, elicit a positive reaction in people's consciences. If the consecrated life maintains its prophetic impact, it serves as a Gospel leaven within a culture, purifying and perfecting it. This is demonstrated by the lives of many saints who in different periods of history were able to immerse themselves in their time without being overcome by it, but opening new paths to the people of their generation. The Gospel way of life is an important source for proposing a new cultural model. A great many founders and foundresses perceiving certain needs of their time, with all the limitations which they themselves recognized, have given these needs an answer which has become an innovative cultural proposal.

Communities of religious institutes and of societies of apostolic life can, in fact, offer concrete and effective cultural proposals when they bear witness to the evangelical manner of practicing mutual acceptance in diversity and of exercising authority, and when they give an example of sharing material and spiritual goods, of being truly international, of cooperating with other institutes, and of listening to the men and women of our time. The manner of thinking and acting of those who follow Christ more closely gives rise to *a true and proper point of reference for culture*; it serves to point out all that is inhuman; it bears witness that God alone strengthens and perfects values. In turn, a genuine inculturation will help consecrated persons to live the radical nature of the Gospel according to the charism of their institute and the character of the people with whom they come into contact. This fruitful relationship can give rise to ways of life and pastoral approaches which can bring enrichment to the whole institute, provided that they are consistent with the founding charism and with the unifying action of the Holy Spirit. In this process, which entails discernment, courage, dialogue, and the challenge of the Gospel, a guarantee of being on the right path is offered by the Holy See, whose task it is to encourage the evangelization of cultures, as well as to authenticate developments and to sanction results in the area of inculturation.[202] This is "a difficult and delicate task, since it raises the question of the Church's fidelity to the Gospel and the Apostolic Tradition amid the constant evolution of cultures."[203]

The new evangelization

81. If the great challenges which modern history poses to the new evangelization are to be faced successfully, what is needed above all is a consecrated life which is continually

open to challenge by the revealed word and the signs of the times.[204] The memory of the great evangelizers, both men and women, who were themselves profoundly evangelized, shows that in order to face the world of today it is necessary to have people who are lovingly dedicated to the Lord and his Gospel. "Consecrated persons, because of their specific vocation, are called to manifest the unity between self-evangelization and witness, between interior renewal and apostolic fervor, between being and acting, showing that dynamism arises always from the first element of each of these pairs."[205]

The new evangelization, like that of all times, will be effective if it proclaims from the rooftops what it has first lived in intimacy with the Lord. It calls for strong personalities, inspired by saintly fervor. The new evangelization demands that consecrated persons have *a thorough awareness of the theological significance of the challenges of our time.* These challenges must be weighed with careful joint discernment, with a view to renewing the mission. Courage in proclaiming the Lord Jesus must be accompanied by trust in Providence, which is at work in the world and which "orders everything, even human differences, for the greater good of the Church."[206]

Important elements enabling institutes to play a successful part in new evangelization are fidelity to the founding charism, communion with all those who in the Church are involved in the same undertaking, especially the bishops, and cooperation with all people of good will. All this requires a careful discernment of the calls which the Holy Spirit makes to each institute, whether in areas where no great immediate progress is foreseen or in other areas where a consoling rebirth is anticipated. In every place and circumstance, consecrated persons should be zealous heralds of Jesus Christ, ready to respond with the wisdom of the Gospel to the questions posed today by the anxieties and the urgent needs of the human heart.

Preference for the poor and the promotion of justice

82. At the beginning of his ministry, in the synagogue at Nazareth Jesus announces that the Spirit has consecrated him to preach good news to the poor, to proclaim release to captives, to give sight back to the blind, to set the oppressed free, to declare a year of favor from the Lord (cf. Lk 4:16–19). Taking up the Lord's mission as her own, the Church proclaims the Gospel to every man and woman, committing herself to their integral salvation. But with special attention, in a true "preferential option," she turns to those who are *in situations of greater weakness*, and therefore in greater need. "The poor," in varied states of affliction, are the oppressed, those on the margin of society, the elderly, the sick, the young, any and all who are considered and treated as "the least."

The option for the poor is inherent in the very structure of love lived in Christ. All of Christ's disciples are therefore held to this option, but those who wish to follow the Lord more closely, imitating his attitudes, cannot but feel involved in a very special way. The sincerity of their response to Christ's love will lead them to live a life of poverty and to embrace the cause of the poor. For each institute, according to its charism, this involves *adopting a simple and austere way of life*, both as individuals and as a community. Strengthened by this living witness and in ways consistent with their choice of life, and maintaining their independence vis-à-vis political ideologies, consecrated persons will be able to denounce the injustices committed against so many sons and daughters of God, and commit themselves to the promotion of justice in the society where they work.[207] In this way, even in present circumstances, through the witness of countless consecrated persons, there will be a renewal of that dedication which was characteristic of the founders and foundresses who spent their lives serving the Lord in the poor. Christ "is poor on earth in the person of his poor. . . . As God he is rich, as man he is poor. With his humanity he has gone up to heaven and, prosperous, is seated at the right hand of the Father, and yet, here on earth, still poor, he suffers hunger, thirst, and nakedness."[208]

The Gospel is made effective through charity, which is the Church's glory and the sign of her faithfulness to the Lord. This is demonstrated by the whole history of the consecrated life, which can be considered a living exegesis of Jesus' words: "As you did it to one of the least of these my brethren, you did it to me" (Mt 25:40). Many institutes, especially in modern times, were established precisely to address one or other of the needs of the poor. But even when such a purpose was not the determining factor, concern and care for the needy—expressed in prayer, assistance, and hospitality—was always a normal part of every form of the consecrated life, even of the contemplative life. And how could it be otherwise, since the Christ encountered in contemplation is the same who lives and suffers in the poor? In this sense, the history of the consecrated life is rich with marvelous and sometimes ingenious examples. Saint Paulinus of Nola, after distributing his belongings to the poor in order to consecrate himself fully to God, built the cells of his monastery above a hospice for the poor. He rejoiced at the thought of this singular "exchange of gifts": the poor, whom he helped, strengthened with their prayers the very "foundations" of his house, wholly dedicated to the praise of God.[209] Saint Vincent de Paul, for his part, loved to say that, when one is obliged to leave prayer to attend to a poor person in need, that prayer is not really interrupted, because "one leaves God to serve God."[210]

Serving the poor is an act of evangelization and, at the same time, a seal of Gospel authenticity and a catalyst for permanent conversion in the consecrated life, since, as Saint Gregory the Great says, "when charity lovingly stoops to provide even for the smallest needs of our neighbor, then does it suddenly surge upward to the highest peaks. And when in great kindness it bends to the most extreme needs, then with much vigor does it resume its soaring to the heights."[211]

Care of the sick

83. Following a glorious tradition, a great number of consecrated persons, above all women, carry out their apostolate in the field of health care, according to the charism of their respective institutes. Down the centuries, many consecrated persons *have given their lives* in service to victims of contagious diseases, confirming the truth that dedication to the point of heroism belongs to the prophetic nature of the consecrated life.

The Church looks with admiration and gratitude upon the many consecrated persons who, by caring for the sick and the suffering, contribute in a significant way to her mission. They carry on the ministry of mercy of Christ, who "went about doing good and healing all" (Acts 10:38). In the footsteps of the Divine Samaritan, physician of souls and bodies,[212] and following the example of their respective founders and foundresses, those consecrated persons committed to this ministry by the charism of their institute should persevere in their witness of love toward the sick, devoting themselves to them with profound understanding and compassion. They should give a special place in their ministry to the poorest and most abandoned of the sick, such as the elderly, and those who are handicapped, marginalized, or terminally ill, and to the victims of drug abuse and the new contagious diseases. Consecrated persons should encourage the sick themselves to offer their sufferings in communion with Christ, crucified and glorified for the salvation of all.[213] Indeed they should strengthen in the sick the awareness of being able *to carry out a pastoral ministry of their own* through the specific charism of the cross, by means of their prayer and their testimony in word and deed.[214]

Moreover, the Church reminds consecrated men and women that a part of their mission is *to evangelize the health-care centers* in which they work, striving to spread the light of Gospel values to the way of living, suffering, and dying of the people of our day. They should endeavor to make the practice of medicine more human, and increase their knowledge of bioethics at the service of the Gospel of life. Above all therefore they should foster respect for the person and for human life from conception to its natural end, in full conformity with the moral teaching of the Church.[215] For this purpose they should set up centers of formation[216] and cooperate closely with those ecclesial bodies entrusted with the pastoral ministry of health care.

Ponder

In this chapter, John Paul II turns to the wide topic of mission. Just as Jesus and the three apostles had to come down from the mountain of the transfiguration, so must we. On the mountaintop we may have enjoyed the comforting presence of the Lord in prayer. But the time comes when, still abiding in prayer, we descend and set out on our own mission.

Mission is not something added on to the consecrated life, as if it were an extra. The phrase "consecration for mission" emphasizes that the very idea of mission is bound up with the consecrated life itself. As the Pope says, "consecrated life itself is a mission" (no. 72).

Many of the ideas in this chapter relate to the way John Paul II presented the theological basis for consecrated life in Chapter 1. They underscore his profound Trinitarian insight, noted in number 18, that the way Jesus lived on earth expressed his relationship to the Father and to the Holy Spirit. Those who seek to imitate him also live a life rooted in the Trinity and actually make Christ present in the world: ". . . they become, day after day, *conformed to Christ*, the prolongation in history of a special presence of the Risen Christ" (no. 19).

Making Christ present in the world is the core of mission. Despite the wide diversity of apostolic works that consecrated persons carry out, all of them in some way make Christ present in the world. It's worthwhile to think about how the concept of presence is central to mission. God became present to the human race in the Incarnation, so much so that God actually became one of us. In Jesus Christ, God draws near to us. Baptism draws us into the death and resurrection of Christ so that we become his members. He lives in us through grace.

As the Church spreads throughout the world, this presence of Christ through faith and the sacraments is spread to more and more people. The term "incarnational reality" expresses this well. In some sense the Church makes the Incarnation present throughout the world in all ages. In *Lumen Gentium*, the Council noted how the Church presents Christ to the world through the lives of religious: "The Church thus portrays Christ in contemplation on the mountain, in his proclamation of the Kingdom of God to the multitudes, in his healing of the sick and maimed, in his work of converting sinners. . . ." (no. 46). For consecrated persons, mission is a form of spiritual fruitfulness by which they, through Christ, bring life to the world.

1. John Paul II wrote that "the mission consists in making Christ present to the world through personal witness" and that this is "the primary task" of the consecrated life (no. 72). How does this primary task underlie the many forms of mission that consecrated persons carry out?

2. After reading this section of *Vita Consecrata*, re-read number 22 in light of the idea of consecration for mission. Consider how the consecration of Jesus was at the root of his mission. Everything he did became a source of grace for us, as John Paul II says: "His perfect offering confers an aspect of consecration upon all the events of

his earthly existence." How does the offering of consecrated persons give everything they do an aspect of mission? How does this outlook help to transform ordinary tasks, even if they are tiresome, into offerings of love?

3. Pope John Paul II mentions several areas of particular importance for mission: the new evangelization, inculturation, promoting justice, the option for the poor, care of the sick, etc. He also mentions that the mission strengthens consecrated life (no. 78). What are some ways or specific examples of how being involved in mission can draw religous out of themselves and help make them a gift of self to others?

Pray

Prayer is closely linked to mission. An intense prayer life will bear fruit in bringing Christ to others. If you are able to spend some time in Eucharistic adoration, bring to the Lord all the people whom you hope to serve in your own mission. Spread out their needs before him and intercede for these persons with trust. Intercessory prayer is a way of being present to others through Christ.

Act

All of us are called to a life of service and self-giving love. Is there an area in your community or family where you have held back and let others do the work? In what way can you relieve their burdens?

II. A Prophetic Witness
in the Face of Great Challenges

The prophetic character of the consecrated life

84. The prophetic character of the consecrated life was strongly emphasized by the Synod Fathers. It takes the shape of *a special form of sharing in Christ's prophetic office*, which the Holy Spirit communicates to the whole People of God. There is a prophetic dimension which belongs to the consecrated life as such, resulting from the radical nature of the following of Christ and of the subsequent dedication to the mission characteristic of the consecrated life. The sign value, which the Second Vatican Council acknowledges in the consecrated life,[217] is expressed in prophetic witness to the primacy which God and the truths of the Gospel have in the Christian life. Because of this pre-eminence nothing can come before personal love of Christ and of the poor in whom he lives.[218]

The Patristic tradition has seen a model of monastic religious life in Elijah, courageous prophet and friend of God.[219] He lived in God's presence and contemplated his passing by in silence; he interceded for the people and boldly announced God's will; he defended God's sovereignty and came to the defense of the poor against the powerful of the world (cf. 1 Kg 18–19). In the history of the Church, alongside other Christians, there have been men and women consecrated to God who, through a special gift of the Holy Spirit, have carried out a genuinely prophetic ministry, speaking in the name of God to all, even to the pastors of the Church. *True prophecy is born of God*, from friendship with him, from attentive listening to his word in the different circumstances of history. Prophets feel in their hearts a burning desire for the holiness of God and, having heard his word in the dialogue of prayer, they proclaim that word with their lives, with their lips and with their actions, becoming people who speak for God against evil and sin. Prophetic witness requires the constant and passionate search for God's will, for self-giving, for unfailing communion in the Church, for the practice of spiritual discernment and love of the truth. It is also expressed through the denunciation of all that is contrary to the divine will and through the exploration of new ways to apply the Gospel in history, in expectation of the coming of God's Kingdom.[220]

Significance for the contemporary world

85. In our world, where it often seems that the signs of God's presence have been lost from sight, a convincing prophetic witness on the part of consecrated persons is increasingly necessary. In the first place this should entail *the affirmation of the primacy of God and of eternal life*, as evidenced in the following and imitation of the chaste, poor, and obedient Christ, who was completely consecrated to the glory of God and to the love of his brethren. The fraternal life is itself prophetic in a society which, sometimes without realizing it, has a profound yearning for a brotherhood which knows no borders. Consecrated persons are being asked to bear witness everywhere with the boldness of a prophet who is unafraid of risking even his life.

Prophecy derives a particularly persuasive power from *consistency between proclamation and life*. Consecrated persons will be faithful to their mission in the Church and the world, if they can renew themselves constantly in the light of the word of God.[221] Thus will they be able to enrich the other faithful with the charismatic gifts they have received and, in turn, let themselves be challenged by the prophetic stimulus which comes from other sectors of the Church. In this exchange of gifts, guaranteed by *full harmony with the Church's Magisterium and discipline*, there will shine forth the action of the Holy Spirit who "gives [the Church] a unity of fellowship and service; he furnishes and directs her with various gifts, both hierarchical and charismatic."[222]

Faithfulness to the point of martyrdom

86. In this century, as in other periods of history, consecrated men and women have borne witness to Christ the Lord *with the gift of their own lives*. Thousands of them have been forced into the catacombs by the persecution of totalitarian regimes or of violent groups, or have been harassed while engaged in missionary activity, in action on behalf of the poor, in assisting the sick and the marginalized; yet they lived and continue to live their consecration in prolonged and heroic suffering, and often with the shedding of their blood, being perfectly configured to the crucified Lord. The Church has already officially recognized the holiness of some of these men and women, honoring them as martyrs for Christ. They enlighten us by their example; they intercede that we may be faithful, and they await us in glory.

There is a widespread desire that the memory of so many witnesses to the faith will remain in the consciousness of the

Church as an invitation to celebrate and imitate them. The institutes of consecrated life and the societies of apostolic life can contribute to this endeavor by *gathering the names* of all those consecrated persons who deserve to be inscribed in the martyrology of the twentieth century, and by compiling *testimonies about them*.[223]

The major challenges facing the consecrated life

87. The prophetic task of the consecrated life is brought into play by *three major challenges* addressed to the Church herself: they are the same challenges as ever, posed in new ways, and perhaps more radically, by contemporary society, at least in some parts of the world. These challenges relate directly to the evangelical counsels of chastity, poverty, and obedience, impelling the Church, and consecrated persons in particular, to clarify and testify to the *profound anthropological significance* of the counsels. The decision to follow the counsels, far from involving an impoverishment of truly human values, leads instead to their transformation. The evangelical counsels should not be considered as a denial of the values inherent in sexuality, in the legitimate desire to possess material goods, or to make decisions for oneself. Insofar as these inclinations are based on nature, they are good in themselves. Human beings, however, weakened as they are by original sin, run the risk of acting on them in a way which transgresses the moral norms. The profession of chastity, poverty, and obedience is a warning not to underestimate the wound of original sin and, while affirming the value of created goods, *it relativizes them* by pointing to God as the absolute good. Thus, while

those who follow the evangelical counsels seek holiness for themselves, they propose, so to speak, a spiritual "therapy" for humanity, because they reject the idolatry of anything created and in a certain way they make visible the living God. The consecrated life, especially in difficult times, is a blessing for human life and for the life of the Church.

The challenge of consecrated chastity

88. The *first challenge* is that of a *hedonistic culture* which separates sexuality from all objective moral norms, often treating it as a mere diversion and a consumer good and, with the complicity of the means of social communication, justifying a kind of idolatry of the sexual instinct. The consequences of this are before everyone's eyes: transgressions of every kind, with resulting psychic and moral suffering on the part of individuals and families. The *reply* of the consecrated life is above all in the *joyful living of perfect chastity*, as a witness to the power of God's love manifested in the weakness of the human condition. The consecrated person attests that what many have believed impossible becomes, with the Lord's grace, possible and truly liberating. Yes, in Christ it is possible to love God with all one's heart, putting him above every other love, and thus to love every creature with the freedom of God! This testimony is more necessary than ever today, precisely because it is so little understood by our world. It is offered to everyone—young people, engaged couples, husbands and wives, and Christian families—in order to show that *the power of God's love can accomplish great things* precisely within the context of human love. It is a

witness which also meets a growing need for interior honesty in human relationships.

The consecrated life must present to today's world examples of chastity lived by men and women who show balance, self-mastery, an enterprising spirit, and psychological and affective maturity.[224] Thanks to this witness, human love is offered a stable point of reference: the pure love which consecrated persons draw from the contemplation of Trinitarian love, revealed to us in Christ. Precisely because they are immersed in this mystery, consecrated persons feel themselves capable of a radical and universal love, which gives them the strength for the self-mastery and discipline necessary in order not to fall under the domination of the senses and instincts. Consecrated chastity thus appears as a joyful and liberating experience. Enlightened by faith in the Risen Lord and by the prospect of the new heavens and the new earth (cf. Rev 21:1), it offers a priceless incentive in the task of educating to that chastity which corresponds to other states of life as well.

The challenge of poverty

89. *Another challenge* today is that of a *materialism which craves possessions*, heedless of the needs and sufferings of the weakest, and lacking any concern for the balance of natural resources. The *reply* of the consecrated life is found in the profession of *evangelical poverty*, which can be lived in different ways and is often expressed in an active involvement in the promotion of solidarity and charity. How many institutes devote themselves to education, training, and professional

formation, preparing young people and those no longer young to become builders of their own future! How many consecrated persons give themselves without reserve in the service of the most disadvantaged people on earth! How many of them work to train future educators and leaders of society, so that they in turn will be committed to eliminating structures of oppression and to promoting projects of solidarity for the benefit of the poor! Consecrated persons fight to overcome hunger and its causes; they inspire the activities of voluntary associations and humanitarian organizations; and they work with public and private bodies to promote a fair distribution of international aid. Nations truly owe a great deal to these enterprising agents of charity, whose tireless generosity has contributed and continues to contribute greatly to making the world more human.

Evangelical poverty at the service of the poor

90. Even before being a service on behalf of the poor, *evangelical poverty is a value in itself*, since it recalls the first of the Beatitudes in the imitation of the poor Christ.[225] Its primary meaning, in fact, is to attest that God is the true wealth of the human heart. Precisely for this reason evangelical poverty forcefully challenges the idolatry of money, making a prophetic appeal as it were to society, which in so many parts of the developed world risks losing the sense of proportion and the very meaning of things. Thus, today more than in other ages, the call of evangelical poverty is being felt also among those who are aware of the scarcity of the planet's resources and who invoke respect for and the conservation of

creation by reducing consumption, by living more simply, and by placing a necessary brake on their own desires.

Consecrated persons are therefore asked to bear a renewed and vigorous evangelical witness to self-denial and restraint, in a form of fraternal life inspired by principles of simplicity and hospitality, also as an example to those who are indifferent to the needs of their neighbor. This witness will of course be accompanied by a *preferential love for the poor* and will be shown especially by sharing the conditions of life of the most neglected. There are many communities which live and work among the poor and the marginalized; they embrace their conditions of life and share in their sufferings, problems, and perils.

Outstanding pages in the history of evangelical solidarity and heroic dedication have been written by consecrated persons in these years of profound changes and great injustices, of hopes and disappointments, of striking victories and bitter defeats. And pages no less significant have been written and are still being written by very many other consecrated persons, who live to the full their life "hid with Christ in God" (Col 3:3) for the salvation of the world, freely giving of themselves, and spending their lives for causes which are little appreciated and even less extolled. In these various and complementary ways, the consecrated life shares in the radical poverty embraced by the Lord, and fulfills its specific role in the saving mystery of his Incarnation and redeeming death.[226]

The challenge of freedom in obedience

91. The *third challenge* comes from those *notions of freedom* which separate this fundamental human good from its

essential relationship to the truth and to moral norms.[227] In effect, the promotion of freedom is a genuine value, closely connected with respect for the human person. But who does not see the aberrant consequences of injustice and even violence, in the life of individuals and of peoples, to which the distorted use of freedom leads?

An effective response to this situation is the *obedience which marks the consecrated life.* In an especially vigorous way this obedience reproposes the obedience of Christ to the Father and, taking this mystery as its point of departure, testifies *that there is no contradiction between obedience and freedom.* Indeed, the Son's attitude discloses the mystery of human freedom as the path of obedience to the Father's will, and the mystery of obedience as the path to the gradual conquest of true freedom. It is precisely this mystery which consecrated persons wish to acknowledge by this particular vow. By obedience they intend to show their awareness of being children of the Father, as a result of which they wish to take the Father's will as their daily bread (cf. Jn 4:34), as their rock, their joy, their shield, and their fortress (cf. Ps 18:2). Thus they show that they are growing in the full truth about themselves, remaining in touch with the source of their existence and therefore offering this most consoling message: "The lovers of your law have great peace; they never stumble" (Ps 119:165).

Carrying out together the Father's will

92. This testimony of consecration takes on special meaning in religious life because of *the community dimension* which marks it. The fraternal life is the privileged place in

which to discern and accept God's will, and to walk together with one mind and heart. Obedience, enlivened by charity, unites the members of an institute in the same witness and the same mission, while respecting the diversity of gifts and individual personalities. In community life which is inspired by the Holy Spirit, each individual engages in a fruitful dialogue with the others in order to discover the Father's will. At the same time, together they recognize in the one who presides an expression of the fatherhood of God and the exercise of authority received from God, at the service of discernment and communion.[228]

Life in community is thus the particular sign, before the Church and society, of the bond which comes from the same call and the common desire—notwithstanding differences of race and origin, language, and culture—to be obedient to that call. Contrary to the spirit of discord and division, authority and obedience shine like a sign of that unique fatherhood which comes from God, of the brotherhood born of the Spirit, of the interior freedom of those who put their trust in God, despite the human limitations of those who represent him. Through this obedience, which some people make their rule of life, the happiness promised by Jesus to "those who hear the word of God and keep it" (Lk 11:28) is experienced and proclaimed for the good of all. Moreover, those who obey have the guarantee of truly taking part in the mission, of following the Lord and not pursuing their own desires or wishes. In this way we can know that we are guided by the Spirit of the Lord, and sustained, even in the midst of great hardships, by his steadfast hand (cf. Acts 20:22–23).

A decisive commitment to the spiritual life

93. One of the concerns frequently expressed at the Synod was that the consecrated life should be nourished *from the wellspring of a sound and deep spirituality*. This is a primary requirement, inscribed in the very essence of the consecrated life by the fact that, just as every other baptized person, and indeed even more so, those who profess the evangelical counsels must aspire with all their strength to the perfection of charity.[229] This commitment is clearly evidenced in the many examples of holy founders and foundresses, and of so many consecrated persons who have borne faithful witness to Christ to the point of martyrdom. To tend toward holiness: this is in summary the program of every consecrated life, particularly in the perspective of its renewal on the threshold of the third millennium. The starting point of such a program lies in leaving everything behind for the sake of Christ (cf. Mt 4:18–22, 19:21, 27; Lk 5:11), preferring him above all things, in order to share fully in his Paschal Mystery.

Saint Paul understood this well when he said: "Indeed I count everything as loss because of the surpassing worth of knowing Christ Jesus my Lord . . . that I may know him and the power of his resurrection" (Phil 3:8, 10). This is the path marked out from the beginning by the apostles, as testified to in the Christian tradition of the East and the West: "Those who now follow Jesus, leaving everything for his sake, remind us of the apostles who, in answer to his invitation, gave up everything. As a result, it has become traditional to speak of religious life as *apostolica vivendi forma*."[230] The same tradition has also emphasized in the consecrated life the aspect of a particular covenant with God, indeed of a spousal covenant with Christ, of which Saint Paul was a master by his example (cf. 1 Cor 7:7) and by his teaching, proposed under the Spirit's guidance (cf. 1 Cor 7:40).

We may say that the spiritual life, understood as life in Christ or life according to the Spirit, presents itself as a path of increasing faithfulness, on which the consecrated person is guided by the Spirit and configured by him to Christ, in full communion of love and service in the Church.

All these elements, which take shape in the different forms of the consecrated life, give rise to *a specific spirituality*, that is, a concrete program of relations with God and one's surroundings, marked by specific spiritual emphases and choices of apostolate, which accentuate and re-present one or another aspect of the one mystery of Christ. When the Church approves a form of consecrated life or an institute, she confirms that in its spiritual and apostolic charism are found all the objective requisites for achieving personal and communal perfection according to the Gospel.

The spiritual life must therefore have first place in the program of families of consecrated life, in such a way that every institute and community will be a school of true evangelical spirituality. Apostolic fruitfulness, generosity in love of the poor, and the ability to attract vocations among the younger generation depend on this priority and its growth in personal and communal commitment. It is precisely *the spiritual quality of the consecrated life* which can inspire the men and women of our day, who themselves are thirsting for absolute values. In this way the consecrated life will become an attractive witness.

Listening to the word of God

94. The word of God is the first source of all Christian spirituality. It gives rise to a personal relationship with the living God and with his saving and sanctifying will. It is for this reason that from the very beginning of institutes of consecrated life, and in a special way in monasticism, what is called *lectio divina* has been held in the highest regard. By its means the word of God is brought to bear on life, on which it projects the light of that wisdom which is a gift of the Spirit. Although the whole of Sacred Scripture is "profitable for teaching" (2 Tim 3:16), and is "the pure and perennial source of spiritual life,"[231] the writings of the New Testament deserve special veneration, especially the Gospels, which are "the heart of all the Scriptures."[232] It is therefore of great benefit for consecrated persons to meditate regularly on the Gospel texts and the New Testament writings which describe the words and example of Christ and Mary and the *apostolica vivendi forma*. Founders and foundresses were inspired by these texts in accepting their vocation and in discerning the charism and mission of their institutes.

Meditation of the Bible *in common* is of great value. When practiced according to the possibilities and circumstances of life in community, this meditation leads to a joyful sharing of the riches drawn from the word of God, thanks to which brothers or sisters grow together and help one another to make progress in the spiritual life. Indeed it would be helpful if this practice were also encouraged among other members of the People of God, priests and laity alike. This will lead, in ways proper to each person's particular gifts, to setting up schools of prayer, of spirituality and of prayerful reading of the Scriptures, in which God "speaks to people as friends (cf. Ex 33:11; Jn 15:14–15) and lives among them (cf. Bar 3:38), so that he may invite and draw them into fellowship with himself." [233]

As the Church's spiritual tradition teaches, meditation on God's word, and on the mysteries of Christ in particular, gives rise to fervor in contemplation and the ardor of apostolic activity. Both in contemplative and active religious life it has always been men and women of prayer, those who truly interpret and put into practice the will of God, who do great works. From familiarity with God's word they draw the light needed for that individual and communal discernment which helps them to seek the ways of the Lord in the signs of the times. In this way they acquire *a kind of supernatural intuition*, which allows them to avoid being conformed to the mentality of this world, but rather to be renewed in their own mind, in order to discern God's will about what is good, perfect, and pleasing to him (cf. Rom 12:2).

In communion with Christ

95. An indispensable means of effectively sustaining communion with Christ is assuredly *the Sacred Liturgy*, and especially the celebration of the Eucharist and the Liturgy of the Hours.

In the first place, the *Eucharist* "contains the Church's entire spiritual wealth, that is, Christ himself, our Passover and living bread, who, through his very flesh, made vital and vitalizing by the Holy Spirit, offers life" to the human family.[234] This is the heart of the Church's life, and also of the consecrated life. How can those who are called, through the profession of the evangelical counsels, to choose Christ as the only meaning of their lives, not desire to establish an ever more profound communion with him by sharing daily in the sacrament which makes him present, in the sacrifice which actualizes the gift of his love on Golgotha, the banquet which nourishes and sustains God's pilgrim people? By its very nature the Eucharist is at the center of the consecrated life, both for individuals and for communities. It is the daily viaticum and source of the spiritual life for the individual and for the institute. By means of the Eucharist all consecrated persons are called to live Christ's Paschal Mystery, uniting themselves to him by offering their own lives to the Father through the Holy Spirit. Frequent and prolonged adoration of Christ present in the Eucharist enables us in some way to relive Peter's experience at the transfiguration: "It is well that we are here." In the celebration of the mystery of the Lord's Body and Blood, the unity and charity of those who have consecrated their lives to God are strengthened and increased.

Alongside the Eucharist, and intimately connected with it, the Liturgy of the Hours, celebrated in union with the prayer of the Church, either in community or individually according to the nature of each institute, expresses the call proper to consecrated persons to raise their hearts in praise and intercession.

The Eucharist is also closely connected with the commitment to continual conversion and necessary purification which consecrated persons bring to maturity in the *sacrament of Reconciliation.* By their frequent encounter with God's mercy, they purify and renew their hearts, and through the humble recognition of their sins achieve openness in their relationship with him. The joyful experience of sacramental forgiveness, on the journey shared with one's brothers and sisters, makes the heart eager to learn and encourages growth in faithfulness.

Confident and humble recourse to *spiritual direction* is of great help on the path of fidelity to the Gospel, especially in the period of formation and at certain other times in life. Through it individuals are helped to respond with generosity to the movements of the Spirit, and to direct themselves resolutely toward holiness.

Finally, I exhort all consecrated persons, according to their own traditions, to renew daily their spiritual union with the Blessed Virgin Mary, reliving with her the mysteries of her Son, especially by saying the rosary.

Ponder

As a prophet, Jesus Christ gave testimony to God first of all through the witness of his life, and also with his words. Consecrated persons are called to do the same. Witness of life takes precedence, however, because spoken words carry no weight if they are not put into practice.

John Paul II notes that the evangelical witness of chastity, poverty, and obedience is especially important in today's world. Great challenges arise in each area, such as hedonism, materialism, and false notions of freedom. One concept that can help us meet these challenges is an idea John Paul II spoke of in his theology of the body: the freedom of the gift. God is Gift, and we receive our life and very being from him as a gift. Our task is to be aware of this and receive those gifts gratefully. It doesn't mean to be passive, for we can and should be active and develop ourselves. Then we can, in turn, make a gift of ourselves to others.

The opposite of receiving is grasping, taking something for ourselves because we think we are entitled to it. This kind of grasping is the root of sin. Genesis speaks of how Adam and Eve saw that the forbidden fruit was desirable, and they reached out and grasped it because they thought they were entitled to it, no matter what God had said. Beneath the grasping is a fundamental distrust of God, a belief that God doesn't truly care about us, so we can't trust him. In a world caught up with grasping, the evangelical counsels of chastity, poverty, and obedience point out a different way: the freedom of the gift.

This freedom helps us not only to offer our own gift of self to others, but to receive their gift as well. A communion of persons is thus formed, in which mission can become a mutual enrichment. Teachers, for example, can certainly recount many stories of what they've learned from their students. This doesn't undercut the prophetic character of the consecrated life. But it does remind us that those who receive the mission are also persons made in the image and likeness of God, who deserve respect and service. The saints understood this truth and sometimes made dramatic gestures in that spirit, such as when Saint Francis kissed the leper.

Because freedom is so important to people today, John Paul II speaks about how obedience in the consecrated life does not contradict freedom. He refers to "the mystery of obedience as the path to the gradual conquest of true freedom" (no. 91). As a philosopher, John Paul II had carefully analyzed the idea of freedom. Because we are persons with free will, we are our own masters. Each of us can say, "No one can will for me." As the Pope puts it, "No one else can will in my stead. No one can substitute his act of the will for mine."*
Even God respects our freedom and does not force our free will, but invites us to love. In marriage, the spouses don't own each other but form a union of persons based on love. Out of love, they give themselves to each other and sacrifice some of

---

* Karol Wojtyla, *Love and Responsibility*, trans. Gregorz Ignatik (Boston: Pauline Books & Media, 2013), p. 6.

their autonomy for the sake of the beloved. Persons can belong to each other only through such love, because in loving they make a self-gift to each other. That is true spousal love.

With the vow of obedience, consecrated persons also act out of true spousal love, but in their case this love is directed to God. In religious consecration, love moves the person to want to give up one's autonomy for the sake of the beloved—God. In doing this religious are not impoverished but enriched, spiritually speaking. "For love makes the person want precisely to give himself to another person—to the one he loves. He wants, so to speak, to stop being his own exclusive possession and to become the possession of the other."[*] This profound idea of freedom can certainly deepen our understanding of obedience.

1. How do the challenges of hedonism, materialism, and false notions of freedom spring from a desire to grasp something for ourselves apart from God? How do the counsels foster, instead, the "freedom of the gift"?

2. In this section John Paul II also speaks of the importance of the spiritual life and prayer. Why is prayer so essential to the consecrated life?

3. How does meditation on the Word of God in a spirit of listening give rise to a personal relationship with God? (see no. 94)

---

* Ibid., p. 108.

Pray

The consecrated life can be seen as "a spousal covenant with Christ" (no. 93). The Pope presents Saint Paul as a model for this by his teaching and example. Take some time to read and prayerfully ponder 1 Corinthians 7:7–40. Ask the Holy Spirit to stir up in your heart the love that seeks only to "please the Lord" (1 Cor 7:32).

Act

What role does Mary play in your life? John Paul II recommends the Rosary as one way of bringing Mary into our life as disciples. Consider how you might grow in your relationship with her. Some ideas are to make or renew a total consecration to her, to renew various forms of Marian prayer, and to bring her more consciously into one's mission and outreach to others.

III. Some New Fields of Mission

Presence in the world of education

96. The Church has always recognized that education is an essential dimension of her mission. The Master of her inner life is the Holy Spirit, who penetrates the innermost depths of every human heart and knows the secret unfolding of history. The whole Church is enlivened by the Holy Spirit and with him carries out her educational work. Within the Church, however, consecrated persons have a specific duty. They are called to bring to bear on the world of education their radical witness to the values of the Kingdom, proposed to everyone in expectation of the definitive meeting with the Lord of history. Because of their special consecration, their particular experience of the gifts of the Spirit, their constant listening to the word of God, their practice of discernment, their rich heritage of pedagogical traditions built up since the establishment of their institute, and their profound grasp of spiritual truth (cf. Eph 1:17), consecrated persons are able to be especially effective in educational activities and to offer a specific contribution to the work of other educators.

Equipped with this charism, consecrated persons can give life to educational undertakings permeated by the Gospel spirit of freedom and charity, in which young people are helped to mature humanly under the action of the Spirit.[235] In this way a community of learning becomes an experience of grace, where the teaching program contributes to uniting into a harmonious whole the human and the divine, the Gospel and culture, faith and life.

The history of the Church, from antiquity down to our own day, is full of admirable examples of consecrated persons who have sought and continue to seek holiness through their involvement in education, while at the same time proposing holiness as the goal of education. Indeed, many of them have achieved the perfection of charity through teaching. This is one of the most precious gifts which consecrated persons today can offer to young people, instructing them in a way that is full of love, according to the wise counsel of Saint John Bosco: "Young people should not only be loved, but should also know that they are loved."[236]

Need for a renewed commitment in the field of education

97. With respectful sensitivity and missionary boldness, consecrated men and women should show that faith in Jesus Christ enlightens the whole enterprise of education, never disparaging human values but rather confirming and elevating them. Thus do consecrated persons become witnesses and instruments of the power of the Incarnation and the vitality of the Spirit. This task of theirs is one of the most significant manifestations of that motherhood which the Church, in the image of Mary, exercises on behalf of all her children.[237]

It is for this reason that the Synod emphatically urged consecrated persons to take up again, wherever possible, the mission of education in schools of every kind and level, and in universities and institutions of higher learning.[238] Making my own the proposal of the Synod, I warmly invite members of institutes devoted to education to be faithful to their founding charism and to their traditions, knowing that the preferential love for the poor finds a special application in the choice of means capable of freeing people from that grave form of poverty which is the lack of cultural and religious training.

Because of the importance that Catholic and ecclesiastical universities and faculties have in the field of education and evangelization, institutes which are responsible for their direction should be conscious of their responsibility. They should ensure the preservation of their unique Catholic identity in complete fidelity to the Church's Magisterium, all the while engaging in active dialogue with present-day cultural trends. Moreover, depending on the circumstances, the members of these institutes and societies should readily become involved in the educational structures of the State. Members of secular institutes in particular, because of their specific calling, are called to this kind of cooperation.

Evangelizing culture

98. Institutes of consecrated life have always had great influence in the formation and transmission of culture. This was true in the Middle Ages, when monasteries became places for the study of the cultural riches of the past, and for the development of a new humanistic and Christian culture. The same has happened every time the light of the Gospel has spread to new nations and peoples. Many consecrated persons have been promoters of culture, and frequently have studied and defended indigenous cultures. The need to contribute to the promotion of culture and to the dialogue between culture and faith is deeply felt in the Church today.[239]

Consecrated persons cannot fail to feel challenged by this pressing need. In their proclamation of the word of God, they too are called to discover the methods most suited to the needs of the different social groups and various professional categories, so that the light of Christ will penetrate all sectors of society and the leaven of salvation will transform society from within, fostering the growth of a culture imbued with Gospel values.[240] At the threshold of the third Christian millennium, such a commitment will enable consecrated men and women to renew their response to the will of God, who reaches out to all those who, knowingly or not, are searching for the Truth and the Life (cf. Acts 17:27).

But in addition to this service of others, within the consecrated life itself there is a need for *a renewed and loving commitment to the intellectual life*, for dedication to study as a means of integral formation and as a path of asceticism which is extraordinarily timely, in the face of present-day cultural diversity. A lessened commitment to study can have grave consequences for the apostolate, by giving rise to a sense of marginalization and inferiority, or encouraging superficiality and rash initiatives.

With all respect for the diversity of charisms and the actual resources of individual institutes, the commitment to study cannot be limited to initial formation or to the gaining of academic degrees and professional qualifications. Rather, study is an expression of the unquenchable desire for an ever deeper knowledge of God, the source of light and all human truth. Consequently, a commitment to study does not isolate consecrated persons in an abstract intellectualism, or confine them within a suffocating narcissism; rather, it is an incentive to dialogue and cooperation, a training in the capacity for judgment, a stimulus to contemplation and prayer in the constant quest for the presence and activity of God in the complex reality of today's world.

When they allow themselves to be transformed by the Holy Spirit, consecrated persons can broaden the horizons of narrow human aspirations and at the same time understand more deeply people and their life stories, going beyond the most obvious but often superficial aspects. Countless challenges are today emerging in the world of ideas, in new areas as well as those in which the consecrated life has traditionally been present. There is an urgent need to maintain fruitful contacts with all cultural realities, with a watchful and critical attitude, but also with confident attention to those who face the particular difficulties of intellectual work, especially when, in response to the unprecedented problems of our times, new efforts of analysis and synthesis have to be attempted.[241] A serious and effective evangelization of these new areas where culture is developed and transmitted cannot take place without active cooperation with the laity involved in them.

Presence in the field of social communications

99. Just as in the past consecrated persons successfully used all kinds of means at the service of evangelization and skillfully met difficulties, today too they are challenged anew by the need to bear witness to the Gospel through the communications media. The media, thanks to impressive developments in technology, have reached every corner of the earth.

Consecrated persons, especially those who have the institutional charism of working in this field, have a duty to learn the language of the media, in order to speak effectively of Christ to our contemporaries, interpreting their "joys and hopes, their griefs and anxieties,"[242] and thus contributing to the building up of a society in which all people sense that they are brothers and sisters making their way to God.

Nevertheless, it is necessary to be vigilant with regard to the distorted use of the media, especially given their extraordinary power of persuasion. The problems which can result for the consecrated life should not be ignored; instead they should be faced with careful discernment.[243] The Church's response is above all educational: it aims at promoting a correct understanding of the dynamics underlying the media and a careful ethical assessment of their programs, as well as the development of healthy habits in their use.[244] In this work of education, aimed at training discerning listeners and expert communicators, consecrated persons are called to offer their specific witness regarding the relative nature of all created realities. In this way they help people to use the media wisely and in accordance with God's plan, but also to free themselves from an obsessive interest in "the form of this world, which is passing away" (1 Cor 7:31).

All efforts in this important new field of the apostolate should be encouraged, so that the Gospel of Christ may be proclaimed also through these modern means. The various institutes should be ready to cooperate, by contributing resources and personnel, in order to implement joint projects in all sectors of social communications. Furthermore, consecrated persons, especially members of secular institutes, should willingly lend their help, wherever pastorally appropriate, for the religious formation of leaders and workers in the field of public and private social communications. This should be done in order to offset the inappropriate use of the media and to promote higher quality programs, the contents of which will be respectful of the moral law and rich in human and Christian values.

IV. Engaged in Dialogue with Everyone

At the service of Christian unity

100. Christ's prayer to the Father before his passion, that his disciples may be one (cf. Jn 17:21–23), lives on in the Church's prayer and activity. How can those called to the consecrated life not feel themselves involved? The wound of disunity still existing between believers in Christ and the urgent need to pray and work for the promotion of Christian unity were deeply felt at the Synod. The ecumenical sensitivity of consecrated persons is heightened also by the awareness that in other Churches and Ecclesial Communities monasticism has been preserved and is flourishing, as is the case in the Eastern Churches, and that there is a renewal of the profession of the evangelical counsels, as in the Anglican Communion and in the Communities of the Reformation.

The Synod emphasized the close connection between the consecrated life and the cause of ecumenism, and the urgent need for a more intense witness in this area. Since the soul of ecumenism is prayer and conversion,[245] institutes of consecrated life and societies of apostolic life certainly have a special duty to foster this commitment. There is an urgent need for consecrated persons to give more space in their lives to ecumenical prayer and genuine evangelical witness, so that by the power of the Holy Spirit the walls of division and prejudice between Christians can be broken down.

Forms of ecumenical dialogue

101. Sharing of the *lectio divina* in the search for the truth, a participation in common prayer, in which the Lord assures us of his presence (cf. Mt 18:20), the dialogue of friendship and charity which makes us feel how pleasant it is when brothers dwell in unity (cf. Ps 133), cordial hospitality shown to brothers and sisters of the various Christian confessions, mutual knowledge and the exchange of gifts, cooperation in common undertakings of service and of witness: these are among the many forms of ecumenical dialogue. They are actions pleasing to our common Father, which show the will to journey together toward perfect unity along the path of truth and love.[246] Likewise, the knowledge of the history, doctrine, liturgy, and charitable and apostolic activity of other Christians cannot but help to make ecumenical activity ever more fruitful.[247]

I wish to encourage those institutes which, either because they were founded for this purpose or because of a later calling, are dedicated to promoting Christian unity and therefore foster initiatives of study and concrete action. Indeed, no institute of consecrated life should feel itself dispensed from working for this cause. My thoughts likewise turn to the

Eastern Catholic Churches with the hope that also through the monastic life of both men and women—the flourishing of which is a grace to be constantly prayed for—they may help to bring about unity with the Orthodox Churches, through the dialogue of charity and the sharing of a common spirituality, itself the heritage of the undivided Church of the first millennium.

In a special way, I entrust to the monasteries of contemplative life the spiritual ecumenism of prayer, conversion of heart, and charity. To this end I encourage their presence wherever Christian communities of different confessions live side by side, so that their total devotion to the "one thing needful" (cf. Lk 10:42)—to the worship of God and to intercession for the salvation of the world, together with their witness of evangelical life according to their special charisms—will inspire everyone to abide, after the image of the Trinity, in that unity which Jesus willed and asked of the Father for all his disciples.

Interreligious dialogue

102. Because "interreligious dialogue is a part of the Church's evangelizing mission,"[248] institutes of consecrated life cannot exempt themselves from involvement also in this field, each in accordance with its own charism and following the directives of ecclesiastical authority. The first form of evangelization in relation to our brothers and sisters of other religions should be the testimony of a life of poverty, humility, and chastity, imbued with fraternal love for all. At the same

time, the freedom of spirit proper to the consecrated life will favor that "dialogue of life"[249] which embodies a basic model of mission and of the proclamation of Christ's Gospel. In order to foster reciprocal knowledge, respect, and charity, religious institutes can also promote *appropriate forms of dialogue*, marked by cordial friendship and mutual sincerity, with the monastic communities of other religions.

Another area for cooperation with men and women of different religious traditions is that of a shared *concern for human life*, extending from compassion for those who are suffering physically and spiritually to commitment to justice, peace, and the protection of God's creation. In these areas, institutes of active life especially will seek an understanding with members of other religions, through that "dialogue of action"[250] which prepares the way for more profound exchanges.

A particular field for successful common action with people of other religious traditions is that of *efforts to promote the dignity of women*. In view of the equality and authentic complementarity of men and women, a valuable service can be rendered above all by consecrated women.[251]

These and other ways in which consecrated persons are engaged in the service of interreligious dialogue require an appropriate training, both in initial formation and in continuing formation. They require study and research,[252] since in this very delicate area a profound knowledge of Christianity and of other religions is needed, accompanied by solid faith and by spiritual and personal maturity.

Spirituality as a response to the search for the sacred and the desire for God

103. Because of the very nature of their choice, all who embrace the consecrated life, men and women alike, become privileged partners in the search for God which has always stirred the human heart and has led to the different forms of asceticism and spirituality. Today, in many places, this search is insistently emerging as a response to cultural forces which tend to marginalize the religious dimension of life, if not actually to deny it.

When consecrated persons live consistently and fully their freely assumed commitments, they are able to offer a response to the longings of their contemporaries, and can help to free them from solutions which are for the most part illusory and often involve a denial of the saving Incarnation of Christ (cf. 1 Jn 4:2–3), such as those proposed, for example, by the sects. By practicing a personal and communal asceticism which purifies and transfigures their entire existence, they bear witness, against the temptation to self-centeredness and sensuality, to the true nature of the search for God. They constitute a warning against confusing that search with a subtle search for self or a flight into gnosticism. Every consecrated person is committed to strengthening the interior life, which in no way involves withdrawal from reality or a turning in upon oneself. Listening in obedience to the word, of which the Church is the guardian and interpreter, the consecrated person points to Christ loved above all things and to the mystery of the Trinity as the response to the profound longings of the human heart and the ultimate goal of every religious journey sincerely open to transcendence.

For this reason, consecrated persons are in duty bound to offer a generous welcome and spiritual support to all those who, moved by a thirst for God and a desire to live the demands of faith, turn to them.[253]

Ponder

The last two parts of this chapter are linked. The new fields of mission discussed in Chapter III can readily be used in the dialogue that John Paul II urges everyone to undertake. Among the new fields of mission, the Pope highlights education. Catholic education has always been a very important mission. It involves a "radical witness to the values of the Kingdom" (no. 96). While the fields of mission in which consecrated persons work often improve living conditions for many, and that is very important, they also open up the horizon to eternal life "in expectation of the definitive meeting with the Lord of history" (no. 96).

John Paul II also emphasizes the importance of evangelizing culture and using the means of social communication. These two fields go hand-in-hand, because the new communication technologies are changing culture. Since 1996, when *Vita Consecrata* was written, the explosion of the Internet has had vast effects. The Vatican has issued two documents specifically on the Internet, stressing that the Church sees the media as gifts that can be put to good use for the Gospel.* It is striking to note that John Paul II not only urges the creation of media that shows forth the Gospel, but that he also encourages education in the healthy use of media. He calls on consecrated persons

---

* Pontifical Council for Social Communications, *The Church and Internet*, February 28, 2002, and *Ethics in Internet*, February 28, 2002.

in particular to lead in educating others to engage in media in a wise, Christ-centered way. As media become ever more an inescapable part of our lives, they also become the field in which much of our discipleship is lived out.

The new media not only offer many opportunities for evangelizing, but also are changing the way evangelization is carried out. "Already, the two-way interactivity of the Internet is blurring the old distinction between those who communicate and those who receive what is communicated, and creating a situation in which, potentially at least, everyone can do both. This is not the one-way, top-down communication of the past."[*] Evangelizers are called to a greater dialogue with people today, who are not so willing to accept statements but demand evidence and proof. Of course, evangelization has always involved communication, but today we are overwhelmed with technology. One of the challenges is to know how to keep the personal dimension alive in the midst of digital products and systems.

The Pope also speaks of dialogue at the service of Christian unity. This can take place in ecumenical discussions with Christians of other faith traditions. Prayer plays an important role in this task. Throughout his papacy, John Paul II was very much concerned with ecumenism and his hopes to achieve Christian unity. In his encyclical *Ut Unum Sint (That They May Be One)*, issued on May 25, 1995, he stressed the Catholic Church's commitment to ecumenism.

---

[*] *The Church and Internet*, no. 6.

In *Vita Consecrata* he also urges dialogue with followers of other religions. Some possible areas of cooperation include respect for human life and the promotion of the dignity of women. Many initiatives have taken place, and consecrated religious are often very active in helping to bring about this kind of fruitful dialogue.

1. How does the Internet, particularly social media, affect the way you communicate with others? In what ways can these tools be used to evangelize?

2. In number 98 the Pope speaks of dedication to study and a renewed commitment to the intellectual life. This should be understood in a broad sense as learning from everything in life, not only in relation to formal education. If you're not attending school right now, what are some ways you can keep your mind active and learn from life experiences?

3. Which field of mission are you most closely involved in? How can you apply to your own life the general guidelines on mission that the Pope offers in this chapter?

PRAY

In view of the dialogue we are called to carry on with everyone, take some time to prayerfully ponder the prayer Jesus offered on the night before his passion (Jn 17:20–25).

ACT

If you have the opportunity to take part in dialogue with others whose religious beliefs might differ from yours, do so, seeking to understand better their point of view. If not, you could act on John Paul II's words to "understand more deeply people and their life stories" (no. 98) by simply taking the time to listen to someone who would like to speak to you.

Conclusion

Unbounded generosity

104. Many people today are puzzled and ask: What is the point of the consecrated life? Why embrace this kind of life, when there are so many urgent needs in the areas of charity and of evangelization itself, to which one can respond even without assuming the particular commitments of the consecrated life? Is the consecrated life not a kind of "waste" of human energies which might be used more efficiently for a greater good, for the benefit of humanity and the Church?

These questions are asked more frequently in our day, as a consequence of a utilitarian and technocratic culture which is inclined to assess the importance of things and even of people in relation to their immediate "usefulness." But such questions have always existed, as is eloquently demonstrated by the Gospel episode of the anointing at Bethany: "Mary took a pound of costly ointment of pure nard and anointed the feet of Jesus and wiped his feet with her hair, and the house was filled with the fragrance of the ointment" (Jn 12:3). When Judas, using the needs of the poor as an excuse, complained about such waste, Jesus replied: "Let her alone!" (Jn 12:7).

This is the perennially valid response to the question which many people, even in good faith, are asking about the relevance of the consecrated life: Could one not invest one's life in a more efficient and reasonable way for the betterment of society? This is how Jesus replies: "Let her alone!" Those who have been given the priceless gift of following the Lord Jesus more closely consider it obvious that he can and must be loved with an undivided heart, that one can devote to him one's whole life, and not merely certain actions or occasional moments or activities. The precious ointment poured out as a pure act of love, and thus transcending all "utilitarian" considerations, is a sign of *unbounded generosity*, as expressed in a life spent in loving and serving the Lord, in order to devote oneself to his person and his Mystical Body. From such a life "poured out" without reserve there spreads a fragrance which fills the whole house. The house of God, the Church, today no less than in the past, is adorned and enriched by the presence of the consecrated life.

What in people's eyes can seem a waste is, for the individuals captivated in the depths of their heart by the beauty and goodness of the Lord, an obvious response of love, a joyful expression of gratitude for having been admitted in a unique way to the knowledge of the Son and to a sharing in his divine mission in the world.

"If any of God's children were to know and taste divine love, the uncreated God, the incarnate God, the God who endured suffering, the God who is the supreme good, they would give themselves completely to him, they would withdraw not only from other creatures but even from their very selves, and with all their being would love this God of love, to the point of being completely transformed into the God-man, who is the supreme Beloved."[254]

The consecrated life in the service of the Kingdom of God

105. "What would become of the world if there were no religious"?[255] Beyond all superficial assessments of its usefulness, the consecrated life is important precisely in its being *unbounded generosity and love*, and this all the more so in a world which risks being suffocated in the whirlpool of the ephemeral. "Without this concrete sign there would be a danger that the charity which animates the entire Church would grow cold, that the salvific paradox of the Gospel would be blunted, and that the 'salt' of faith would lose its savor in a world undergoing secularization."[256] The Church and society itself need people capable of devoting themselves totally to God and to others for the love of God.

The Church can in no way renounce the consecrated life, for it *eloquently expresses her inmost nature as "Bride."* In the consecrated life the proclamation of the Gospel to the whole world finds fresh enthusiasm and power. There is a need for people able to show the fatherly face of God and the motherly face of the Church, people who spend their lives so that others can have life and hope. The Church needs consecrated persons who, even before committing themselves to the service of this or that noble cause, allow themselves to be transformed by God's grace and conform themselves fully to the Gospel.

The whole Church finds in her hands this great gift and gratefully devotes herself to promoting it with respect, with prayer, and with the explicit invitation to accept it. It is important that bishops, priests, and deacons, convinced of the evangelical superiority of this kind of life, should strive to discover and encourage the seeds of vocation through preaching, discernment, and wise spiritual guidance. All the faithful are asked to pray constantly for consecrated persons, that their fervor and their capacity to love may grow continually and thus contribute to spreading in today's society the fragrance of Christ (cf. 2 Cor 2:15). The whole Christian community—pastors, laity, and consecrated persons—is responsible for the consecrated life and for welcoming and supporting new vocations.[257]

To young people

106. To you, young people, I say: if you hear the Lord's call, do not reject it! Dare to become part of the great movements of holiness which renowned saints have launched in their following of Christ. Cultivate the ideals proper to your age, but readily accept God's plan for you if he invites you to seek holiness in the consecrated life. Admire all God's works in the world, but be ready to fix your eyes on the things destined never to pass away.

The third millennium awaits the contribution of the faith and creativity of great numbers of young consecrated persons, that the world may be made more peaceful and able to welcome God and, in him, all his sons and daughters.

To families

107. I address you, Christian families. Parents, give thanks to the Lord if he has called one of your children to the consecrated life. It is to be considered a great honor—as it always has been—that the Lord should look upon a family and choose to invite one of its members to set out on the path of the evangelical counsels! Cherish the desire to give the Lord one of your children so that God's love can spread in the world. What fruit of conjugal love could be more beautiful than this?

We must remember that if parents do not live the values of the Gospel, the young man or woman will find it very difficult to discern the calling, to understand the need for the sacrifices which must be faced, and to appreciate the beauty of the goal to be achieved. For it is in the family that young people have their first experience of Gospel values and of the love which gives itself to God and to others, They also need to be trained in the responsible use of their own freedom, so that they will be prepared to live, as their vocation demands, in accordance with the loftiest spiritual realities.

I pray that you, Christian families, united with the Lord through prayer and the sacramental life, will create homes where vocations are welcomed.

To men and women of good will

108. To all the men and women who are willing to listen to my voice, I wish to address an invitation to seek the paths

which lead to the living and true God, including the path marked out by the consecrated life. Consecrated persons bear witness to the fact that "whoever follows after Christ, the perfect man, becomes himself more of a man."[258] How many consecrated men and women have bent down, and continue to bend down, as Good Samaritans, over the countless wounds of the brothers and sisters whom they meet on their way!

Look at these people seized by Christ, who show that in self-mastery, sustained by grace and God's love, lies the remedy for the craving to possess, to seek pleasure, to dominate. Do not forget the charisms which have shaped remarkable "seekers of God" and benefactors of humanity, who have provided sure paths for those who seek God with a sincere heart. Consider the great number of saints who have flourished in this way of life; consider the good done to the world, in the past and in the present, by those who have devoted themselves to God! Does not this world of ours need joyful witnesses and prophets of the beneficent power of God's love? Does it not also need men and women who, by their lives and their work, are able to sow seeds of peace and fraternity?[259]

To consecrated persons

109. But it is above all to you, consecrated women and men, that at the end of this Exhortation I appeal with trust: live to the full your dedication to God, so that this world may never be without a ray of divine beauty to lighten the path of human existence. Christians, immersed in the cares and concerns of this world but also called to holiness, need to discover

in you purified hearts which in faith "see" God, people docile to the working of the Holy Spirit who resolutely press on in fidelity to the charism of their call and mission.

You know well that you have set out on a journey of continual conversion, of exclusive dedication to the love of God and of your brothers and sisters, in order to bear ever more splendid witness to the grace which transfigures Christian life. The world and the Church seek authentic witnesses to Christ. And the consecrated life is a gift which God offers in order that everyone can recognize the "one thing necessary" (cf. Lk 10:42). To bear witness to Christ by one's life, works, and words is the particular mission of the consecrated life in the Church and in the world.

You know the one in whom you have put your trust (cf. 2 Tim 1:12): give him everything! Young people will not be deceived: when they come to you, they want to see what they do not see elsewhere. An immense task awaits you in the future: in a special way young consecrated persons, by witnessing to their consecration, can lead their contemporaries to a renewal of their lives.[260] An impassioned love of Jesus Christ is a powerful attraction for those other young people whom Christ in his goodness is calling to follow him closely and for ever. Our contemporaries want to see in consecrated persons the joy which comes from being with the Lord.

Consecrated women and men, old and young alike, live faithfully your commitment to God, in mutual edification and mutual support! Despite the difficulties you may occasionally encounter, and despite the lessening of esteem for the consecrated life in certain quarters, you have the task of once more inviting the men and women of our time to lift their eyes, not to let themselves be overwhelmed by everyday things, to let themselves be captivated by the fascination of God and of his Son's Gospel. Do not forget that you, in a very special way, can and must say that you not only belong to Christ but that "you have become Christ"![261]

Looking to the future

110. You have not only a glorious history to remember and to recount, but also *a great history still to be accomplished*! Look to the future, where the Spirit is sending you in order to do even greater things.

Make your lives a fervent expectation of Christ; go forth to meet him like the wise virgins setting out to meet the Bridegroom. Be always ready, faithful to Christ, the Church, to your institute, and to the men and women of our time.[262] In this way you will day by day be renewed in Christ, in order with his Spirit to build fraternal communities, to join him in washing the feet of the poor, and to contribute in your own unique way to the transfiguration of the world.

As it enters the new Millennium, may our world, entrusted to human hands, become ever more human and just, a sign and anticipation of the world to come, in which the Lord, humble and glorified, poor and exalted, will be the full and lasting joy for us and for our brothers and sisters, together with the Father and the Holy Spirit.

Prayer to the Holy Trinity

111. Most Holy Trinity, blessed and the source of all blessedness, bless your sons and daughters whom you have called to praise the greatness of your love, your merciful goodness, and your beauty.

Father Most Holy, sanctify the sons and daughters who have consecrated themselves to you, for the glory of your name. Enfold them with your power, enabling them to bear witness that you are the origin of all things, the one source of love and freedom. We thank you for the gift of the consecrated life, which in faith seeks you and in its universal mission invites all people to draw near to you.

Jesus our Savior, Incarnate Word, as you have entrusted your own way of life to those whom you have called, continue to draw to yourself men and women who will be, for the people of our time, dispensers of mercy, heralds of your return, living signs of the resurrection and of its [treasures of virginity, poverty, and obedience].* May no tribulation separate them from you and from your love!

Holy Spirit, Love poured into our hearts, who grants grace and inspiration to our minds, the perennial source of life, who brings to fulfillment the mission of Christ by means of many charisms, we pray to you for all consecrated persons. Fill their hearts with the deep certainty of having been chosen to love,

---

* The bracketed words appear in the English version on the Vatican website. However, they are not in the other languages nor in the official Latin, which reads: *futurae resurrectionis vivi indices bonorum*; living signs of the goods of the future resurrection. *Ed.*

to praise, and to serve. Enable them to savor your friendship; fill them with your joy and consolation; help them to overcome moments of difficulty and to rise up again with trust after they have fallen; make them mirrors of the divine beauty. Give them the courage to face the challenges of our time and the grace to bring to all mankind the goodness and loving kindness of our Savior Jesus Christ (cf. Tit 3:4).

Invocation of the Blessed Virgin Mary

112. Mary, image of the Church, the Bride without spot or wrinkle, which by imitating you "preserves with virginal purity an integral faith, a firm hope, and a sincere charity,"[263] sustain consecrated persons on their journey toward the sole and eternal blessedness.

To you, Virgin of the Visitation, do we entrust them, that they may go forth to meet human needs, to bring help, but above all to bring Jesus. Teach them to proclaim the mighty things which the Lord accomplishes in the world, that all peoples may extol the greatness of his name. Support them in their work for the poor, the hungry, those without hope, the little ones and all who seek your Son with a sincere heart.

To you, our Mother, who desire the spiritual and apostolic renewal of your sons and daughters in a response of love and complete dedication to Christ, we address our confident prayer. You who did the will of the Father, ever ready in obedience, courageous in poverty, and receptive in fruitful virginity, obtain from your divine Son that all who have received the gift of following him in the consecrated life may be enabled to bear witness to that gift by their transfigured lives, as they joyfully make their way with all their brothers and sisters toward our heavenly homeland and the light which will never grow dim.

We ask you this: that in everyone and in everything glory, adoration, and love may be given to the Most High Lord of all things, who is Father, Son, and Holy Spirit.

Given in Rome, at Saint Peter's, on March 25, the Solemnity of the Annunciation of the Lord, in the year 1996, the eighteenth of my Pontificate.

Joannes Paulus pp. II

PONDER

It has been a long journey through *Vita Consecrata*. In the conclusion of the document, John Paul II turns to the question that many people ask about the consecrated life: What is its point? Why spend one's life in this manner when it is possible to do good in so many other ways? Is it a waste? All that he has said in this document indicates that the consecrated life is a beautiful gift, and certainly not a waste. But instead of returning to any analysis, the Pope recalls the Gospel scene of Mary of Bethany pouring oil on the feet of Jesus. To those who objected, Jesus gave a simple answer: "Let her alone!" Her action was an outpouring of love, symbolized by the outpouring of the oil. Similarly, the consecrated life is an outpouring of love for Jesus. Even if not all may see the value of this life, the Church can never be without it because it is an important way of love.

Those who follow Christ in consecrated life can do many things, engage in many types of works, and do good to so many people. But ultimately the point is not to *do* but to *love*. The consecrated life is meant to be a life of unbounded love for Jesus. This generous love is poured out on others, too, but even if that weren't possible and one could do nothing but offer up one's sufferings, that would be enough.

A certain mystery remains: the consecrated life is a gift to the Church, yet why are so many reluctant to accept it? The answer, perhaps, is that it is a demanding gift. It is a gift that, when received, calls forth something from the one who accepts it. John Paul II asks everyone in the Church, especially young people and families, but also all people of good will, to better understand this gift and to foster it. Families can create a climate where young people will be better able to hear and appreciate the call to consecrated life. And it is up to consecrated persons themselves to give a joyful witness that will attract new members.

John Paul II concludes his document with an appeal to consecrated men and women: "Live to the full your dedication to God" (no. 109). Doing so will lead to the "transfiguration of the world" (no. 110). Having started out this document with a meditation on the transfiguration of Christ, the Pope brings us to its logical conclusion. Those who have gone up the mountain with Christ, who have seen his glory, are then sent out to the world to bring his love to all: to the poor, to the lonely and forgotten. The light that shone on the face of Christ is a light that continues to shed its radiance to the ends of the earth.

1. How can Christian families help to foster vocations to the consecrated life? In particular, how can parents support their children who may be called to this life?

2. How can we promote a culture of vocation in which all members of the Church are encouraged to think about their life choices in terms of vocation, of what God is calling them to be?

3. After reading *Vita Consecrata*, how has your understanding of the consecrated life grown? What is one main point that you can take away from it?

Pray

Jesus said, "The harvest is plentiful but the laborers are few; therefore ask the Lord of the harvest to send out laborers into his harvest" (Lk 10:2). Prayer is the first and most essential way of promoting vocations to the consecrated life. Take some time to slowly pray the prayer to the Holy Trinity and the invocation of the Blessed Virgin Mary in numbers 111 and 112 of the document.

Act

What can you do to foster vocations to the consecrated life? Could you encourage young people to consider it? Perhaps your parish or diocese has a vocational initiative in which you could participate.

Notes

1. Cf. *Propositio* 2.

2. Second Vatican Ecumenical Council, Decree on the Church's Missionary Activity *Ad Gentes*, 18.

3. Cf. Second Vatican Ecumenical Council, Dogmatic Constitution on the Church *Lumen Gentium*, 44; Paul VI, Apostolic Exhortation *Evangelica Testificatio* (June 29, 1971), 7: *AAS* 63 (1971), 501–502; Apostolic Exhortation *Evangelii Nuntiandi* (December 8, 1975), 69: *AAS* 68 (1976), 59.

4. Cf. *Lumen Gentium*, 44.

5. Cf. John Paul II, Address at the General Audience, September 28, 1994, 5: *L'Osservatore Romano*, September 29, 1994, 4.

6. Cf. *Propositio* 1.

7. Cf. Saint Francis De Sales, *Introduction to the Devout Life*, Part 1, Chapter 3.

8. *Lumen Gentium*, 43.

9. Cf. John Paul II, Homily at the Mass for the conclusion of the Ninth Ordinary General Assembly of the Synod of Bishops (October 29, 1994), 3: *L'Osservatore Romano*, October 30, 1994, 5.

10. Cf. Synod of Bishops, Ninth Ordinary General Assembly, Message of the Synod (October 27, 1994), VII: *L'Osservatore Romano*, October 29, 1994, 7.

11. Cf. *Propositio* 5, B.

12. Cf. Rule, 4, 21; 72, 11.

13. Cf. *Propositio* 12.

14. Cf. *Code of Canons of the Eastern Churches*, canon 570.

15. Cf. Second Vatican Ecumenical Council, Decree on the Appropriate Renewal of the Religious Life *Perfectae Caritatis*, 7; *Ad Gentes*, 40.

16. Cf. *Propositio* 6.

17. Cf. Ibid., 4.

18. Cf. Ibid.,7.

19. Cf. Ibid.,11.

20. Cf. Ibid.,14.

21. Cf. *Code of Canon Law*, canon 605; *Code of Canons of the Eastern Churches*, canon 571; *Propositio* 13.

22. Cf. *Propositio* 3, 4, 6, 7, 8, 10, 13, 28, 29, 30, 35, 48.

23. Cf. *Propositio* 3, A and B.

24. Cf. Ibid., 3, C.

25. Cf. Cassian: *"Secessit tamen solus in monte orate, per hoc scilicet nos instruens suae secessionis exemplo . . . ut similiter secedamus"* (*Collationes* 10, 6: *PL* 49, 827); "Yet still he retired alone in the mountain to pray, teaching us by his example . . . thus also should we retire." Saint Jerome: *"Et Christum quaeras in solitudine et ores solus in monte cum Iesu"* (Epistula ad Paulinum 58, 4, 2: PL 22, 582); "Seek Christ in solitude; pray on the mount alone with Jesus." William of Saint-Thierry: *"[Vita solitaria] ab ipso Domino familiarissime celebrata, ab eius discipulis ipso praesente concupita: cuius transfigurationis gloriam cum vidissent qui cum eo in monte sancto erant, continuo Petrus . . . optimum sibi iudicavit in hoc semper esse"* (*Ad Fratres de Monte Dei*, I, 1: *PL* 184, 310). "[The solitary life] was diligently practiced by the Lord himself, and his disciples desired it even while he was still with them. When those who were with him on the holy mountain saw the glory of his Transfiguration, Peter immediately . . . judged that it would be good for him to always be there."

26. *Lumen Gentium*, 1.

27. Ibid., 44.

28. Cf. Congregation for Religious and Secular Institutes, *Instruction on Essential Elements in the Church's Teaching as Applied to Institutes Dedicated to Works of the Apostolate* (May 31, 1983), 5.

29. Cf. *Summa Theologiae*, II–II, q. 186, a. 1.

30. Cf. *Propositio* 16.

31. Cf. John Paul II, Apostolic Exhortation *Redemptionis Donum* (March 25, 1984), 3: *AAS* 76 (1984), 515–517.

32. Saint Francis of Assisi, *Regula Bullata*, I, 1.

33. *"Tota Trinitas apparuit: Pater in voce; Filius in homine; Spiritus in nube clara";* "The whole Trinity appears: the Father in the voice, the Son in the man, the Holy Spirit in the bright cloud." Saint Thomas Aquinas, *Summa Theologiae*, III, q, 45, a. 4, ad 2.

34. *Perfectae Caritatis*, 1.

35. *Lumen Gentium*, 44.

36. Symeon the New Theologian, *Hymns*, II, verses 19–27: *SCh* 156, 178–179.

37. Cf. John Paul II, Address at the General Audience, November 9, 1994, 4: *L'Osservatore Romano*, November 10, 1994, 4.

38. *Lumen Gentium*, 44.

39. Saint Ignatius of Antioch, *Letter to the Magnesians* 8, 2: *Patres Apostolici*, ed. F. X. Funk, II, 237.

40. Cf. *Propositio* 3.

41. *Expositions on the Book of Psalms*, 44, 3: *PL* 36, 495–496.

42. Cf. *Perfectae Caritatis*, 17.

43. Cf. *Propositio* 25.

44. Cf. *Lumen Gentium*, 42.

45. Ibid., 44.

46. Blessed Elizabeth of the Trinity, *Le ciel dans la foi. Traité Spirituel*, I, 14: *Oeuvres complètes* (Paris, 1991), 106.

47. Cf. Saint Augustine, *Confessions*, I, 1: *CCL* 27, 1.

48. John Paul II, Address at the General Audience, March 29, 1995, 1: *L'Osservatore Romano*, March 30, 1995, 4.

49. Cf. *Lumen Gentium*, 53.

50. Ibid., 46.

51. Cf. *Propositio* 55.

52. *Lumen Gentium*, 44.

53. Cf. *Redemptionis Donum*, *AAS* 76, 522–524.

54. Cf. *Lumen Gentium*, 44; John Paul II, Address at the General Audience, October 26, 1994, 5: *L'Osservatore Romano*, October 27, 1994, 4.

55. *Lumen Gentium*, 42.

56. Cf. Roman Ritual, *Rite of Religious Profession*: Solemn Blessing or Consecration of Professed Men, no. 67, and Solemn Blessing or Consecration of Professed Women, no. 72; Roman Pontifical, *Rite of Consecration to a Life of Virginity*: Solemn Blessing, no. 38; Eucologion Sive Rituale Graecorum, *Officium Parvi Habitum id est Mandiae*, 384–385; Pontificale Iuxta Ritum Ecclesiae Syrorum Occidentalium id Est Antiochiae, *Ordo Rituum Monasticorum* (Vatican City: Vatican Polyglot Press, 1942), 307–309.

57. Cf. Saint Peter Damian, *Liber qui appellatur "Dominus vobiscum" ad Leonem eremitam: PL* 145, 231–252.

58. *Lumen Gentium*, 32; *Code of Canon Law*, canon 208; *Code of Canons of the Eastern Churches*, canon 11.

59. Cf. *Ad Gentes*, 4; *Lumen Gentium*, 4, 12, 13; Pastoral Constitution on the Church in the Modern World *Gaudium et Spes*, 32; Decree on the Apostolate of the Laity *Apostolicam Actuositatem*, 3; John Paul II, Post-Synodal Apostolic Exhortation *Christifideles Laici* (December 30, 1988), 20–21: *AAS* 81 (1989), 425–428; Congregation for the Doctrine of the Faith, Letter to the Bishops of the Catholic Church on Some Aspects of the Church Understood as Communion *Communionis Notio* (May 28, 1992), 15: *AAS* 85 (1993), 847.

60. *Lumen Gentium*, 31.

61. Cf. Ibid., 12; *Christifideles Laici*, 20–21: *AAS* 81 (1989), 425–428.

62. *Lumen Gentium*, 5.

63. Ecumenical Council of Trent, Session XXIV, Canon 10: *DS* 1810; Pius XII, Encyclical Letter *Sacra Virginitas* (March 25, 1954): *AAS* 46 (1954), 176.

64. Cf. *Propositio* 17.

65. *Lumen Gentium*, 41.

66. Cf. ibid., 46.

67. Ibid.

68. Cf. Pius XII, Motu Proprio *Primo Feliciter* (March 12, 1948), 6: *AAS* 40 (1948), 285.

69. *Code of Canon Law*, canon 713 § 1; cf. *Code of Canons of the Eastern Churches*, canon 563 §2.

70. Cf. *Code of Canon Law*, canon 713 § 2. "Clerical members" are specifically addressed in canon 713 §3.

71. *Lumen Gentium*, 31.

72. Saint Theresa of the Child Jesus, *Manuscrits autobiographiques* B, 2 v: "To be your bride, O Jesus . . . to be, in union with you, a mother of souls."

73. Cf. *Perfectae Caritatis*, 8, 10, 12.

74. Synod of Bishops, Second Extraordinary General Assembly, Final Report *Ecclesia sub verbo Dei Mysteria Christi celebrans pro salute mundi* (December 7, 1985), II, A, 4: *Enchiridion Vaticanum* 9, 1753.

75. Synod of Bishops, Ninth Ordinary General Assembly, *Message of the Synod* (October 27, 1994), IX: *L'Osservatore Romano*, (English-language edition), November 2, 1994, 7.

76. Cf. Saint Thomas Aquinas, *Summa Theologiae*, II–II, q. 184, a. 5, ad 2; II–II, q. 186, a. 2, ad 1.

77. Cf. *Libellus de Principiis Ordinis Praedicatorum. Acta Canonizationis Sancti Dominici: Monumenta Ordinis Praedicatorum Historica* 16 (1935), 30.

78. John Paul II, Apostolic Letter *Orientale Lumen* (May 2, 1995), 12: *AAS* 87 (1995), 758.

79. Congregation for Religious and Secular Institutes and Congregation for Bishops, Directives for the Mutual Relations between Bishops and Religious in the Church *Mutuae Relationes* (May 14, 1978), 51: *AAS* 70 (1978), 500.

80. Cf. *Propositio* 26.

81. Cf. Ibid., 27.

82. *Perfectae Caritatis*, 2.

83. *Orientale Lumen*, *AAS* 87 (1995), 762.

84. John Paul II, Apostolic Letter *Tertio Millennio Adveniente* (November 10, 1994), 42: AAS 87 (1995), 32.

85. *Evangelii Nuntiandi*, *AAS* 68 (1976), 58.

86. Cf. *Perfectae Caritatis*, 15; Saint Augustine, *Regula ad Servos Dei*, 1, 1: *PL* 32, 1372.

87. Saint Cyprian, *On the Lord's Prayer*, 23: *PL* 4, 553; cf. *Lumen Gentium*, 4.

88. Cf. *Propositio* 20.

89. Saint Basil, *Long Rule*, Question 7: *PG* 31, 931.

90. Saint Basil, *Short Rule*, Question 225: *PG* 31, 1231.

91. Cf. *Essential Elements in the Church's Teaching as Applied to Institutes Dedicated to Works of the Apostolate*, 51; *Code of Canon Law*, canon 631 § 1; *Code of Canons of the Eastern Churches*, canon 512 §1.

92. Cf. Congregation for Institutes of Consecrated Life and Societies of Apostolic Life, Instruction on Fraternal Life in Community *Congregavit Nos in Unum Christi Amor* (February 2, 1994), 47–53: Rome, 1994, 58–64; *Code of Canon Law*, canon 618; *Propositio* 19.

93. Cf. *Fraternal Life in Community*, 68; *Propositio* 21.

94. Cf. *Propositio* 28.

95. Sacred Congregation for Religious and Secular Institutes, *Document on Religious and Human Promotion* (August 12, 1980), 11, 24: *L'Osservatore Romano*, English-language edition, 4 (January 26, 1981), 11.

96. *Christifideles Laici*, 31–32: *AAS* 81 (1989), 451–452.

97. *Regula Bullata*, I, 1.

98. *Letters* 109, 171, 196.

99. Cf. Rule 13 at the end of the *Spiritual Exercises*.

100. *Sayings*, no. 217.

101. *Manuscrits autobiographiques*, B, 3v.

102. Cf. *Propositio* 30, A.

103. Cf. *Redemptionis Donum*, 15: *AAS* 76 (1984), 541–542.

104. *Lumen Gentium*, 1.

105. *Communionis Notio*, 16: *AAS* 85 (1993), 847–848.

106. Cf. *Lumen Gentium*, 13.

107. Second Vatican Ecumenical Council, Decree on the Bishops' Pastoral Office in the Church *Christus Dominus*, 11.

108. *Mutuae Relationes*, 11: *AAS* 70 (1978), 480.

109. Cf. ibid.

110. Cf. *Code of Canon Law*, canon 576.

111. Cf. *Code of Canon Law*, canon 586; *Mutuae Relationes*, 13: *AAS* 70 (1978), 481–482.

112. Cf. *Ad Gentes*, 18.

113. Cf. *Code of Canon Law*, Canon 586 §2 and 591; *Code of Canons of the Eastern Churches*, Canon 412 §2.

114. Cf. *Propositio* 29, 4.

115. Cf. Ibid., 49, B.

116. Ibid., 54.

117. Cf. *Fraternal Life in Community*, 56.

118. *Apologia to William of Saint Thierry*, IV, 8: *PL* 182, 903–904.

119. Cf. *Perfectae Caritatis*, 23.

120. Cf. *Mutuae Relationes*, 21, 61: *AAS* 70 (1978), 486, 503–504; *Code of Canon Law*, Canons 708–709.

121. Cf. *Perfectae Caritatis*, 1; *Lumen Gentium*, 46.

122. Cf. *Gaudium et Spes*, 4.

123. John Paul II, Message to the Fourteenth Assembly of the Conference of Religious of Brazil (July 11, 1986), 4: *Insegnamenti* IX/2 (1986), 237; cf. *Propositio* 31.

124. *Mutuae Relationes*, 63, 65: *AAS* 70 (1978), 504, 504–505.

125. *Lumen Gentium*, 31.

126. Saint Anthony Mary Zaccaria, *Writings*, Sermon II (Rome 1975), 129.

127. Cf. *Propositio* 33, A and C.

128. Cf. Ibid., 33, B.

129. Cf. *Fraternal Life in Community*, 62; Directives on Formation in Religious Institutes *Potissimum Institutioni* (February 2, 1990), 92–93: *AAS* 82 (1990), 123–124.

130. Cf. *Propositio* 9, A.

131. Cf. Ibid., 9.

132. John Paul II, Encyclical Letter The Gospel of Life *Evangelium Vitae* (March 25, 1995), 99: *AAS* 87 (1995), 514.

133. Congregation for Religious and Secular Institutes, Instruction on the Contemplative Life and on the Enclosure of Nuns *Venite Seorsum* (August 15, 1969), V: *AAS* 61 (1969), 685.

134. Cf. ibid., I: loc. cit., 674.

135. Second Vatican Ecumenical Council, Constitution on the Sacred Liturgy *Sacrosanctum Concilium*, 2.

136. *Lumen Gentium*, 6.

137. Cf. Saint John of the Cross, *Spiritual Canticle*, 29, 1.

138. Cf. *Code of Canon Law*, canon 667 §4; *Propositio* 22, 4.

139. Cf. Paul VI, Motu proprio *Ecclesiae Sanctae* (June 8, 1966), II, 30–31: *AAS* 58 (1966), 780; *Perfectae Caritatis*, 7, 16; *Venite Seorsum*, VI: *AAS* 61 (1969) 686.

140. Cf. Pius XII, Apostolic Constitution *Sponsa Christi* (November 21, 1950) VII: *AAS* 43 (1951), 18–19; *Perfectae Caritatis*, 22.

141. Cf. *Code of Canon Law*, canon 588 §1.

142. Cf. *Perfectae Caritatis*, 10.

143. Cf. ibid., 8, 10.

144. Cf. ibid., 10; *Code of Canon Law*, canon 588 §3.

145. Cf. *Lumen Gentium*, 31.

146. Cf. *Propositio* 8.

147. John Paul II, Address at General Audience, February 22, 1995, 6: *L'Osservatore Romano* (English-language edition), March 1, 1995, 11.

148. Cf. *Perfectae Caritatis*, 10.

149. Cf. *Code of Canon Law*, canon 588 § 2.

150. Cf. *Propositio* 10; *Perfectae Caritatis*, 15.

151. Cf. *Code of Canon Law*, 573; *Code of Canons of the Eastern Churches*, canon 410.

152. Cf. *Propositio* 13, B.

153. Cf. Ibid., 13, C.

154. Cf. Ibid., 13, A.

155. Cf. *Gaudium et Spes*, 48.

156. Cf. *Propositio* 13, B.

157. *Lumen Gentium*, 1.

158. Cf. *Propositio* 24.

159. Cf. *Fraternal Life in Community*, 67.

160. Cf. *Propositio* 48, A.

161. Cf. Ibid., 48, B.

162. Cf. Ibid., 48, C.

163. Cf. Ibid., 49, A.

164. Cf. *Potissimum Institutioni*, 29: *AAS* 82 (1990), 493.

165. Cf. *Propositio* 49, B.

166. Cf. *Essential Elements in the Church's Teaching as Applied to Institutes Dedicated to Works of the Apostolate*, 45.

167. Cf. *Code of Canon Law*, canon 607 §1.

168. Cf. *Propositio* 50.

169. Cf. *Fraternal Life in Community*, 32–33.

170. Cf. *Propositio* 51.

171. Cf. *Fraternal Life in Community*, 43–45.

172. *Potissimum Institutioni*, 70: *AAS* 82 (1990), 513–514.

173. Cf. ibid., 68, l.c., 512.

174. *Lumen Gentium*, 46.

175. Cf. *Propositio* 35, A.

176. *Gaudium et Spes*, 4.

177. Cf. *Lumen Gentium*, 12.

178. Paul VI, Encyclical Letter *Ecclesiam Suam* (August 6, 1964), III: *AAS* 56 (1964), 639.

179. Saint Gregory the Great, *Homilies on Ezekiel*, Book II, II, 11: *PL* 76, 954–955.

180. Saint Augustine, *Sermon* 78, 6: *PL* 38, 492.

181. Cf. Fourth General Conference of the Latin American Episcopate, *New Evangelization, Human Promotion, and Christian Culture* (CELAM, 1992), 178.

182. Conference "On the Spirit of the Society" (February 9, 1653): *Correspondance, Entretiens, Documents*, ed. Coste, Volume IX (Paris, 1923), 592.

183. Cf. *Essential Elements in the Church's Teaching as Applied to Institutes Dedicated to Works of the Apostolate*, 23–24.

184. Cf. Blessed Elizabeth of the Trinity, *O mon Dieu, Trinité que j'adore, Oeuvres Complètes* (Paris, 1991), 199–200.

185. Cf. *Evangelii Nuntiandi*, 69: *AAS* 68 (1976), 59.

186. Cf. *Propositio* 37, A.

187. Cf. *Lumen Gentium*, 46; *Evangelii Nuntiandi*, 69: *AAS* 68 (1976), 59.

188. *Lumen Gentium*, 44, 46.

189. *Ad Gentes*, 18, 40.

190. Letter from Cochin to members of the Society in Rome (January 15, 1544): *Monumenta Historica Societatis Iesu* 67 (1944), 166–167.

191. Cf. *Lumen Gentium*, 44.

192. John Paul II, Encyclical Letter *Redemptoris Missio* (December 7, 1990), 69: *AAS* 83 (1991), 317–318; *Catechism of the Catholic Church*, no. 927.

193. *Redemptoris Missio*, 31: *AAS* 83 (1991), 277.

194. Ibid., 2: loc. cit., 251.

195. *Ad Gentes*, 18; cf. *Redemptoris Missio*, 69: *AAS* 83 (1991), 317–318.

196. Cf. *Propositio* 38.

197. *Redemptoris Missio*, 44: *AAS* 83 (1991), 290.

198. Cf. ibid., 46: loc. cit., 292.

199. Cf. ibid., 52–54: loc. cit., 299–302.

200. Cf. *Propositio* 40, A.

201. *Redemptoris Missio*, 55: *AAS* 83 (1991), 302; Pontifical Council for Interreligious Dialogue and Congregation for the Evangelization of Peoples, Instruction *Dialogue and Proclamation: Reflections and Perspectives* (May 19, 1991), 45–46: *AAS* 84 (1992), 429–430.

202. Cf. *Propositio* 40, B.

203. John Paul II, Post-Synodal Apostolic Exhortation *Ecclesia in Africa* (September 1995), 62: *L'Osservatore Romano*, September 16, 1995, 5.

204. *Evangelii Nuntiandi*, 15: *AAS* 68 (1976), 13–15.

205. Synod of Bishops, Ninth Ordinary General Assembly, *Relatio ante Disceptationem*, 22: *L'Osservatore Romano*, October 3–4, 1994, 12.

206. John XXIII, *Opening Speech to the Second Vatican Ecumenical Council* (October 11, 1962): *AAS* 54 (1962), 789.

207. Cf. *Propositio* 18.

208. Saint Augustine, *Sermon* 123, 3–4: *PL* 38, 685–686.

209. Cf. *Poem XXI* 386–394: *PL* 61, 587.

210. Conference "On the Rules" (May 30, 1647): *Correspondance, Entretiens, Documents*: ed., Coste, Volume IX (Paris, 1923), 319.

211. Saint Gregory the Great, *The Pastoral Rule* 2, 5: *PL* 77, 33.

212. Cf. John Paul II, Apostolic Letter *Salvifici Doloris* (February 11, 1984), 28–30: *AAS* 76 (1984). 242–248.

213. Cf. ibid., 18: loc. cit., 221–224; *Christifideles Laici*, 52–53: *AAS* 81 (1989), 469–500.

214. Cf. John Paul II, Post-Synodal Apostolic Exhortation *Pastores Dabo Vobis* (March 25, 1992), 77: *AAS* 84 (1992), 794–795.

215. Cf. *Evangelium Vitae*, 78–101: *AAS* 87 (1995), 490–518.

216. Cf. *Propositio* 43.

217. Cf. *Lumen Gentium*, 44.

218. John Paul II, Homily at the Closing Liturgy of the Ninth Ordinary General Assembly of the Synod of Bishops (October 29, 1994), 3: *AAS* 87, (1995), 580.

219. Cf. Saint Athanasius, *Life of Saint Anthony*, 7: *PG*, 26, 854

220. Cf. *Propositio* 39, A.

221. Cf. *Propositiones* 15, A and 39, C.

222. *Lumen Gentium*, 4; cf. Decree on the Ministry and Life of Priests *Presbyterorum Ordinis*, 2.

223. Cf. *Propositio* 53; *Tertio Millennio Adveniente*, 37: *AAS* 87 (1995), 29–30.

224. Cf. *Perfectae Caritatis*, 12.

225. Cf. *Propositio* 18, A.

226. Cf. *Perfectae Caritatis*, 13.

227. Cf. John Paul II, Encyclical Letter *Veritatis Splendor* (August 6, 1993), 31–35: *AAS* 85 (1993), 1158–1162

228. Cf. *Propositio* 19, A; *Perfectae Caritatis*, 14.

229. Cf. Ibid., 15.

230. John Paul II, Address at the General Audience, February 8, 1995, 2: *L'Osservatore Romano* (English-language edition), February 15, 1995, 11.

231. Second Vatican Ecumenical Council, Dogmatic Constitution on Divine Revelation *Dei Verbum*, 21; cf. *Perfectae Caritatis*, 6.

232. *Catechism of the Catholic Church*, no. 125; cf. *Dei Verbum*, 18.

233. *Dei Verbum*, 2.

234. *Presbyterorum Ordinis*, 5.

235. Second Vatican Ecumenical Council, Declaration on Christian Education *Gravissimum Educationis*, 8.

236. *Scritti pedagogici e spirituali* (Rome, 1987), 294.

237. Cf. John Paul II, Apostolic Constitution *Sapientia Christiana* (April 15, 1979), II: *AAS* 71 (1979), 471.

238. Cf. *Propositio* 41.

239. Cf. *Sapientia Christiana*, II: *AAS* 71 (1979), 470.

240. Cf. *Propositio* 36.

241. *Gaudium et Spes*, 5.

242. Ibid., 1.

243. Cf. *Fraternal Life in Community*, 34.

244. Message for the 28th World Communications Day (January 24, 1994): *L'Osservatore Romano* (English-language edition), February 2, 1994, 3.

245. Cf. John Paul II, Encyclical Letter *Ut Unum Sint* (May 25, 1995) 21: *AAS* 87 (1995), 934.

246. Cf. ibid., 28: loc. cit., 938–939.

247. Cf. *Propositio* 45.

248. *Redemptoris Missio*, 55: *AAS* 83 (1991), 302.

249. Instruction *Dialogue and Proclamation: Reflections and Perspectives*, 42a: *AAS* 84 (1992), 428.

250. Ibid., 42b: loc. cit.

251. Cf. *Propositio* 46.

252. Instruction *Dialogue and Proclamation: Reflections and Perspectives*, 42c: *AAS* 84 (1992), 428.

253. Cf. *Propositio* 47.

254. Saint Angela of Foligno, *Il libro della Beata Angela da Foligno* (Grottaferrata, 1985), 683.

255. Saint Teresa of Avila, *Autobiography*, Chapter 32, 11.

256. *Evangelica Testificatio*, 3: *AAS* 63 (1971), 498.

257. Cf. *Propositio* 48.

258. *Gaudium et Spes*, 41.

259. Cf. *Evangelica Testificatio*, 53: *AAS* 63 (1971), 524; *Evangelii Nuntiandi*, 69: *AAS* 68 (1976), 59.

260. Cf. *Propositio* 16.

261. Saint Augustine, *Treatise on Saint John's Gospel*, XXI, 8: *PL* 35, 1568.

262. Document on *Religious and Human Promotion*, 13–21.

263. *Lumen Gentium*, 64.

About the Author

 Since 1976, Marianne Lorraine Trouvé, FSP, has been a member of the Daughters of St. Paul, an international congregation of women religious. She has an M.A. in theology from the University of Dayton and has served on the editorial staff of Pauline Books & Media for more than twenty years. Sister Marianne has taught novitiate classes on the theology of consecrated life in the thought of Saint John Paul II. She is the author of several books, including *Mary: Help in Hard Times* and *Angels: Help from on High*. When she's not writing, editing, or working on logic puzzles, Sister Marianne can be found blogging at www.thomasfortoday.blogspot.com.